THE BASIC

COOKING BIBLE

Publications International, Ltd.

Favorite Brand Name Recipes at www.fbnr.com

All recipes and photographs that contain specific brand names are copyrighted by those companies and/or associations, unless otherwise specified. All photographs *except* those on pages 10, 62, 64, 65, 72, 82, 118, 144 and 293 copyright © Publications International, Ltd.

Carnation, Nestlé and Toll House are registered trademarks of Nestlé.

Butter Flavor CRISCO® all-vegetable shortening and Butter Flavor CRISCO® No-Stick Cooking Spray are artificially flavored.

Some of the products listed in this publication may be in limited distribution.

Photography on pages 18, 28, 49, 70, 174, 188, 192, 194, 200, 214, 240, 244 and 280 by Proffitt Photography Ltd., Chicago.

Illustrated by Roberta Polfus.

Pictured on the front cover *(clockwise from top right):* Lemon Melts *(page 302),* Cocoa Cheesecake *(page 208)* and Fettuccine Gorgonzola with Sun-Dried Tomatoes *(page 192).*
Pictured on the back cover *(clockwise from top):* Lazy-Daisy Cake *(page 272),* Beef Teriyaki Stir-Fry *(page 70),* Lots o' Chocolate Bread *(page 214)* and Saucy Tropical Turkey *(page 108).*

ISBN: 1-4127-2071-0

Library of Congress Control Number: 2004110631

Manufactured in China.

8 7 6 5 4 3 2 1

Microwave Cooking: Microwave ovens vary in wattage. Use the cooking times as guidelines and check for doneness before adding more time.

Preparation/Cooking Times: Preparation times are based on the approximate amount of time required to assemble the recipe before cooking, baking, chilling or serving. These times include preparation steps such as measuring, chopping and mixing. The fact that some preparations and cooking can be done simultaneously is taken into account. Preparation of optional ingredients and serving suggestions is not included.

CONTENTS

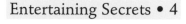

ENTERTAINING SECRETS

As a beginning cook you may feel a little intimidated by the thought of preparing a meal for guests or planning a party. One sure way to look like a pro when entertaining is to serve appetizers as your guests arrive. It's a great way to break the ice if your guests don't know each other—and while they're munching you can sneak off to the kitchen for a few minutes to handle any last-minute dinner details.

No doubt you have questions about starters. What's the difference between appetizers and hors d'oeuvres? Why serve appetizers? Do starters have to be fancy? How do you put together an appetizer party? All of these questions and more are answered in these two pages!

An appetizer is a food served before a meal to stimulate the appetite—it is not meant to satisfy your hunger. (The term may be used interchangeably with the French term "hors d'oeuvre.") A variety of foods, hot or cold, may be served as appetizers. An appetizer can be as simple as a dip with chips or sliced cheese or, as elaborate as Spinach and Cheese Bundles (page 16).

When serving appetizers before a meal, follow these helpful hints:
•One or two selections should be ample, allowing five to seven servings per person.

•Prepare recipes that contrast in temperature, texture and flavor with the meal that follows. For example, Bruschetta al Fresca (page 11) would be a refreshing opener before a main course of roast beef or steak. However, if you are planning an ethnic dinner, preparing an appetizer from the same foreign country would provide a memorable beginning.

•Many people prefer to serve first-course appetizers informally before the guests are seated at the dinner table—this allows the cook time to make last-minute meal preparations. These starters should be easy for your guests to manage—finger foods work best.

ENTERTAINING SECRETS

•Starters such as soup and salad should always be served when guests are seated because they are much too difficult to eat while standing.

For a cocktail party or open house where appetizers are the main event, keep these helpful tips in mind:

•Plan an assortment of savory and sweet snacks, dips and spreads, as well as finger foods (including some that are more hearty and filling).

•Plan on ten to twelve servings per person as a minimum. Remember, the longer the event lasts, the more food your guests will eat.

•Cold appetizers, such as dips and marinated vegetables, should be made at least several hours to one full day ahead since their flavors actually improve with time.

•Some hot appetizers can be cooked ahead of time and simply reheated just before serving, while others are best prepared at the last moment.

•If the food on your appetizer table will be sitting out for several hours, it is very important, for food safety reasons, to maintain the appropriate serving temperatures. Appetizers that need to remain chilled, such as shrimp cocktail, should be served on a platter set over cracked ice. Hot appetizers, such as meatballs or quiche, should be served in a chafing dish, fondue pot or slow cooker to keep them hot. Do not let any foods remain at room temperature for more than two hours.

•Be sure to prepare a balance of hot and cold appetizers that provide a range of flavors and textures, from spicy and rich to light and refreshing.

•Keep in mind that at large parties with limited seating, guests appreciate finger foods and bite-size portions with not-too-drippy sauces.

Part of the fun in serving an array of appetizers is in the presentation. Here are some quick and easy ideas for dressing up your hors d'oeuvres:

•When arranging an appetizer buffet, place the centerpiece towards the back of the table. That way it will not be in the way of guests when they reach for food.

•Hollow out a medium-sized head of red cabbage or a large sweet bell pepper (any color) to use as an attractive "bowl" for a dip. Or, fill a small glass bowl with dip and artfully conceal it with the outer leaves of red or green cabbage or iceberg lettuce before surrounding it with colorful vegetable dippers and crisp crackers.

•For an easy garnish on a spread or casserole, choose one of the recipe's ingredients, for example, red onion, and save a few pretty slices as a special finishing touch to arrange on top.

•A sprinkling of finely chopped fresh herbs, tomato or bell pepper can add much-needed color to almost any dish, such as grilled meats, pasta dishes and creamy soups.

5

SIMPLE STARTERS

spinach-artichoke party cups

Nonstick cooking spray

36 small wonton wrappers (2½ to 3½ inches square)

1 small can (8½ ounces) artichoke hearts, drained and chopped

½ package (10 ounces) frozen chopped spinach, thawed and squeezed dry

1 cup shredded Monterey Jack cheese

½ cup grated Parmesan cheese

½ cup mayonnaise

1 clove garlic, minced

Preheat oven to 300°F. Spray mini muffin pan lightly with cooking spray. Press one wonton wrapper into each cup; spray lightly with cooking spray. Bake about 9 minutes or until light golden brown. Remove shells from muffin pan and set aside to cool. Repeat with remaining wonton wrappers.*

Meanwhile, combine artichoke hearts, spinach, cheeses, mayonnaise and garlic in medium bowl; mix well.

Fill wonton cups with spinach-artichoke mixture (about 1½ teaspoons). Place filled cups on baking sheet. Bake about 7 minutes or until heated through. Serve immediately. *Makes 36 appetizers*

Wonton cups may be prepared up to one week in advance. Cool completely and store in an airtight container.

Tip: If you have leftover spinach-artichoke mixture after filling the wonton cups, place it in a shallow ovenproof dish and bake it at 350°F until hot and bubbly. Serve with bread or crackers.

cucumber-dill dip

Salt

1 cucumber, peeled, seeded and finely chopped

6 green onions, white parts only, chopped

1 package (3 ounces) reduced-fat cream cheese

1 cup plain yogurt

2 tablespoons fresh dill *or* 1 tablespoon dried dill weed

Fresh dill sprigs

1. Lightly salt cucumber in small bowl; toss. Refrigerate 1 hour. Drain cucumber; dry on paper towels. Return cucumbers to bowl and add onions. Set aside.

2. Place cream cheese, yogurt and dill in food processor or blender; process until smooth. Stir into cucumber mixture. Cover; refrigerate 1 hour. Spoon dip into individual plastic cups with lids or glass bowl; garnish with fresh dill sprigs. *Makes about 2 cups dip*

helpful hint

Use the recommended amount of dill in this and any recipe that calls for it. Its distinctive flavor can easily dominate a dish.

fast guacamole and "chips"

2 ripe avocados

½ cup restaurant-style chunky salsa

¼ teaspoon hot pepper sauce (optional)

½ seedless cucumber, sliced into ⅛-inch rounds

1. Cut avocados in half; remove and discard pits. Scoop flesh into medium bowl. Mash with fork.

2. Add salsa and pepper sauce, if desired; mix well.

3. Transfer guacamole to serving bowl; surround with cucumber "chips." *Makes 8 servings, about 1¾ cups*

cucumber-dill dip

california veggie rolls

1 package (8 ounces) cream cheese, softened

½ teaspoon LAWRY'S® Garlic Powder With Parsley

½ teaspoon LAWRY'S® Lemon Pepper

6 large (burrito size) *or* 12 soft taco size flour tortillas, warmed to soften

1 large bunch fresh spinach leaves, cleaned and stems removed

1½ cups (6 ounces) shredded cheddar cheese

1½ cups shredded carrot

Fresh salsa

In small bowl, mix together cream cheese, Garlic Powder With Parsley and Lemon Pepper. On each flour tortilla, spread a layer of cream cheese mixture. Layer on spinach leaves, cheddar cheese and carrot. Roll-up tortilla and secure with toothpick. Slice each roll into 1½-inch pieces. Serve with fresh salsa.

Makes 3 dozen rolls

Variation: Adding sliced deli meat or adding Dijon mustard to the cream cheese will give variety to these rolls.

Hint: To keep tortillas soft until slicing, wrap tightly in plastic wrap or cover with damp towel.

Prep. Time: 20 minutes

california veggie rolls

bruschetta al fresca

1½ cups seeded and
    chopped tomatoes
    (about 2 to
    3 tomatoes)

3 tablespoons chopped
    fresh basil

1 tablespoon balsamic
    vinegar

2 tablespoons olive oil

1 teaspoon LAWRY'S®
    Garlic Salt

1 teaspoon LAWRY'S®
    Seasoned Pepper

1 loaf French baguette
    bread, cut
    diagonally into
    ½-inch slices

LAWRY'S™ Garlic
    Spread, Ready-To-
    Spread

Parmesan cheese,
    shredded

In medium bowl, gently mix together first six
ingredients. Cover and refrigerate to blend flavors for
1 hour or up to 24 hours. On baguette slices evenly
spread Garlic Spread; broil until golden. Top each slice
with 1 tablespoon tomato mixture and garnish with
Parmesan cheese.

Makes about 1½ cups (for about 24 bread slices)

Prep. Time: 15 minutes
Chill Time: 1 to 24 hours
Cook Time: 2 to 3 minutes

helpful hint

*For a refreshing fruit taste with just a hint of
sweetness, we recommend pairing the rich, savory
flavor of this appetizer with White Zinfandel.*

artichoke crostini

1 jar (6 ounces)
   marinated artichoke
   hearts, drained and
   chopped

3 green onions, chopped

5 tablespoons grated
   Parmesan cheese,
   divided

2 tablespoons
   mayonnaise

12 slices French bread
   (½ inch thick)

1. Preheat broiler. Combine artichokes, green onions, 3 tablespoons cheese and mayonnaise in small bowl; mix well.

2. Arrange bread slices on baking sheet. Broil 4 to 5 inches from heat source 2 to 3 minutes on each side or until lightly browned.

3. Remove baking sheet from broiler. Spoon about 1 tablespoon artichoke mixture on each bread slice and sprinkle with remaining 2 tablespoons cheese. Broil 1 to 2 minutes or until cheese is melted and lightly browned. *Makes 4 servings*

Tip: Garnish crostini with red bell pepper, if desired.

Prep and Cook Time: 25 minutes

pesto veggie dip

⅔ cup *French's*® *GourMayo*™ Sun Dried Tomato Mayonnaise

¼ cup sour cream

¼ cup grated Parmesan cheese

3 tablespoons minced fresh basil

1 teaspoon minced garlic

STIR together all ingredients in bowl. Cover and refrigerate for 30 minutes to blend flavors.

SERVE with cut-up vegetables and breadsticks for dipping. *Makes about 1 cup*

Prep Time: 5 minutes
Cook Time: 0 minutes

artichoke crostini

quick and easy stuffed mushrooms

1 slice whole wheat bread

16 large mushrooms

½ cup sliced celery

½ cup sliced onion

1 clove garlic

Nonstick cooking spray

1 teaspoon Worcestershire sauce

½ teaspoon marjoram leaves, crushed

⅛ teaspoon ground red pepper

Dash paprika

1. Tear bread into pieces; place in food processor. Process 30 seconds or until crumbs form. Transfer to small bowl; set aside.

2. Remove stems from mushrooms; reserve caps. Place mushroom stems, celery, onion and garlic in food processor. Process with on/off pulses until vegetables are finely chopped.

3. Preheat oven to 350°F. Coat nonstick skillet with cooking spray. Add vegetable mixture; cook and stir over medium heat 5 minutes or until onion is tender. Remove to bowl. Stir in bread crumbs, Worcestershire sauce, marjoram and ground red pepper.

4. Fill mushroom caps with mixture, pressing down firmly. Place filled caps in shallow baking pan about ½ inch apart. Spray lightly with cooking spray. Sprinkle with paprika. Bake 15 minutes or until hot.

Makes 8 servings

Note: Mushrooms can be stuffed up to 1 day ahead. Refrigerate filled mushroom caps, covered, until ready to serve. Bake in preheated 350°F oven 20 minutes or until hot.

baked garlic bundles

½ of 16-ounce package frozen phyllo dough, thawed to room temperature

¾ cup butter, melted

3 large heads garlic, separated into cloves and peeled

½ cup finely chopped walnuts

1 cup Italian-style bread crumbs

helpful hint

The whole garlic bulb is called a head.

Preheat oven to 350°F. Remove phyllo from package; unroll and place on large sheet of waxed paper. Using scissors, cut phyllo crosswise into 2-inch-wide strips. Cover with large sheet of waxed paper and damp kitchen towel. (Phyllo dries out quickly if not covered.)

Lay 1 phyllo strip on flat surface; brush immediately with melted butter. Place 1 clove of garlic at 1 end of strip. Sprinkle about 1 teaspoon walnuts over length of strip. Roll up garlic clove and walnuts in strip, tucking in side edges as you roll. Brush bundle with melted butter; roll in bread crumbs to coat. Repeat with remaining phyllo strips, garlic cloves, walnuts, butter and bread crumbs until all but smallest garlic cloves are used. Place bundles on rack in shallow roasting pan. Bake 20 minutes or until crispy.

Makes 24 to 27 appetizers

baked garlic bundles

spinach cheese bundles

1 container (6½ ounces) garlic- and herb-flavored spreadable cheese

½ cup chopped fresh spinach

¼ teaspoon black pepper

1 package (17¼ ounces) frozen puff pastry, thawed

Sweet and sour or favorite dipping sauce (optional)

1. Preheat oven to 400°F. Combine spreadable cheese, spinach and pepper in small bowl; mix well.

2. Roll out one sheet puff pastry dough on floured surface into 12-inch square. Cut into 16 (3-inch) squares. Place about 1 teaspoon cheese mixture in center of each square. Brush edges of squares with water. Bring edges together up over filling and twist tightly to seal; fan out corners of puff pastry.

3. Place bundles 2 inches apart on ungreased baking sheet. Bake about 13 minutes or until golden brown. Repeat with remaining sheet of puff pastry and cheese mixture. Serve warm with dipping sauce, if desired.

Makes 32 bundles

BelGioioso® mascarpone cucumber delights

BELGIOIOSO® Mascarpone

Cocktail rye bread

Sliced fresh cucumber

Dill seasoning

Spread BelGioioso Mascarpone on a piece of cocktail rye bread. Place cucumber slice on top and sprinkle with dill seasoning. Arrange on platter and serve as an appetizer.

Makes about 40 appetizers

spinach cheese bundles

spicy chicken bundles

1 pound ground chicken
   or turkey

2 teaspoons minced
   fresh ginger

2 cloves garlic, minced

¼ teaspoon red pepper
   flakes

3 tablespoons soy sauce

1 tablespoon cornstarch

1 tablespoon peanut or
   vegetable oil

⅓ cup finely chopped
   water chestnuts

⅓ cup thinly sliced green
   onions

¼ cup chopped peanuts

12 large lettuce leaves,
   such as romaine

Chinese hot mustard
   (optional)

1. Combine chicken, ginger, garlic and red pepper flakes in medium bowl.

2. Blend soy sauce into cornstarch in cup until smooth.

3. Heat wok or large skillet over medium-high heat. Add oil; heat until hot. Add chicken mixture; stir-fry 2 to 3 minutes or until chicken is no longer pink.

4. Stir soy sauce mixture and add to wok. Stir-fry 30 seconds or until sauce boils and thickens. Add water chestnuts, onions and peanuts; heat through.*

5. Divide filling evenly among lettuce leaves; roll up. Secure with toothpicks. Serve warm or at room temperature. Do not let bundles stand at room temperature more than 2 hours. Serve with hot mustard, if desired. *Makes 12 appetizers*

*Filling may be made ahead to this point; cover and refrigerate up to 4 hours. Just before rolling in lettuce, reheat chicken filling until warm. Proceed as directed in step 5.

spicy chicken bundles

spring rolls

1 cup pre-shredded cabbage or coleslaw mix

½ cup finely chopped cooked ham

¼ cup finely chopped water chestnuts

¼ cup thinly sliced green onions

3 tablespoons plum sauce, divided

1 teaspoon dark sesame oil

3 (6-inch) flour tortillas

Combine cabbage, ham, water chestnuts, onions, 2 tablespoons plum sauce and sesame oil in medium bowl. Mix well. Spread remaining 1 tablespoon plum sauce evenly over tortillas. Spread about ½ cup cabbage mixture on each tortilla to within ¼ inch of edge; roll up. Wrap each tortilla tightly in plastic wrap. Refrigerate at least 1 hour or up to 24 hours before serving. Cut each tortilla diagonally into 4 pieces.

Makes 12 appetizers

garlic cheese bread

2 tablespoons I CAN'T BELIEVE IT'S NOT BUTTER!® Spread-tub or stick

1 clove garlic, finely chopped

1 loaf French or Italian bread (about 12 inches long), halved lengthwise

¼ cup shredded mozzarella cheese (about 2 ounces)

2 tablespoons grated Parmesan cheese

Preheat oven to 350°F.

In small bowl, blend I Can't Believe It's Not Butter!® Spread and garlic. Evenly spread bread with garlic mixture, then sprinkle with cheeses.

On baking sheet, arrange bread and bake 10 minutes or until bread is golden and cheeses are melted. Slice and serve.

Makes 2 servings

four cheese spread

1 package (8 ounces)
   cream cheese,
   softened

1 cup shredded Swiss
   cheese (about
   4 ounces)

1 cup shredded fontina
   or Monterey Jack
   cheese (about
   3 ounces)

½ cup sour cream

¼ cup grated Parmesan
   cheese

¼ cup finely chopped
   fresh basil leaves *or*
   1½ teaspoons dried
   basil leaves, crushed

1 tablespoon finely
   chopped fresh
   parsley

1 tablespoon lemon
   juice

1 envelope LIPTON®
   RECIPE SECRETS®
   Vegetable Soup Mix

Line 4-cup mold or bowl with waxed paper or dampened cheese cloth; set aside.

With food processor or electric mixer, combine all ingredients until smooth. Pack into prepared mold; cover and chill. To serve, unmold onto serving platter and remove waxed paper. Garnish, if desired, with additional chopped parsley and basil. Serve, if desired, with assorted crackers, bagel chips or cucumber slices.

Makes about 3½ cups spread

spanish-style garlic shrimp

4 tablespoons I CAN'T BELIEVE IT'S NOT BUTTER!® Spread, divided

1 pound uncooked medium shrimp, peeled and deveined

½ teaspoon salt

2 cloves garlic, finely chopped

½ to 1 jalapeño pepper, seeded and finely chopped

¼ cup chopped fresh cilantro or parsley

1 tablespoon fresh lime juice

In 12-inch nonstick skillet, melt 1 tablespoon I Can't Believe It's Not Butter!® Spread over high heat and cook shrimp with salt 2 minutes or until shrimp are almost pink, turning once. Remove shrimp and set aside.

In same skillet, melt remaining 3 tablespoons I Can't Believe It's Not Butter!® Spread over medium-low heat and cook garlic and jalapeño pepper, stirring occasionally, 1 minute. Return shrimp to skillet. Stir in cilantro and lime juice and heat 30 seconds or until shrimp turn pink. Serve, if desired, with crusty Italian bread. *Makes 6 servings*

helpful hint

Jalapeño peppers can sting and irritate the skin; wear rubber gloves when handling peppers and do not touch eyes. Wash hands after handling.

spanish-style garlic shrimp

cheesy pepper & onion quesadillas

⅓ cup margarine

3¾ cups frozen stir-fry
vegetable blend
(onions and red,
yellow and green
bell peppers)

¾ teaspoon chili powder

1 package (8 ounces)
fat-free cream
cheese, softened

1 package (8 ounces)
shredded fat-free
Cheddar cheese

10 (6-inch) flour tortillas

Salsa (optional)

1. Preheat oven to 425°F.

2. Heat margarine in large nonstick skillet over medium heat until melted. Add stir-fry blend and chili powder. Cook and stir until tender. Drain, reserving margarine.

3. Beat cream cheese with electric mixer at medium speed until smooth. Add Cheddar cheese, mixing until blended. Spread 2 tablespoons cheese mixture onto each tortilla; top with pepper mixture. Fold tortillas in half; place on baking sheet. Brush with reserved margarine.

4. Bake 10 minutes. Cut each tortilla in half. Serve warm with salsa, if desired. *Makes 20 appetizers*

Prep Time: 10 minutes
Cook Time: 10 minutes

cheesy pepper & onion quesadillas

sesame italian breadsticks

¼ **cup grated Parmesan cheese**

3 **tablespoons sesame seeds**

2 **teaspoons Italian seasoning**

1 **teaspoon kosher salt (optional)**

12 **frozen bread dough dinner rolls, thawed**

¼ **cup butter, melted**

1. Preheat oven to 425°F. Spray large baking sheet with nonstick cooking spray.

2. In small bowl, combine cheese, sesame seeds, Italian seasoning and salt, if desired. Spread out on plate.

3. On lightly floured surface, roll each dinner roll into rope, about 8 inches long and ½ inch thick. Place on baking sheet and brush tops and sides with butter. Roll each buttered rope in cheese mixture, pressing mixture into sides. Return ropes to baking sheet, placing 2 inches apart. Twist each rope 3 times, pressing both ends of rope down on baking sheet. Bake 10 to 12 minutes or until golden brown.

Makes 12 breadsticks

helpful hint

Sesame seeds are widely available packaged in supermarkets and are sold in bulk in specialty stores and ethnic markets. Because of their high oil content, they easily turn rancid and are best stored in the refrigerator where they will keep up to six months or they may be frozen up to a year.

sesame italian breadsticks

stuffed party baguette

2 medium red bell peppers

1 French bread loaf, about 14 inches long

¼ cup plus 2 tablespoons prepared fat-free Italian dressing, divided

1 small red onion, very thinly sliced

8 large fresh basil leaves

3 ounces Swiss cheese, very thinly sliced

1. Preheat oven to 425°F. Cover large baking sheet with foil.

2. To roast bell peppers, cut peppers in half; remove stems, seeds and membranes. Place peppers, cut sides down, on prepared baking sheet. Bake 20 to 25 minutes or until skins are browned, turning occasionally.

3. Transfer peppers from baking sheet to paper bag; close bag tightly. Let stand 10 minutes or until peppers are cool enough to handle and skins are loosened. Using sharp knife, peel off skins; discard skins. Cut peppers into strips.

4. Trim ends from bread; discard. Cut loaf lengthwise in half. Remove soft insides of loaf; reserve removed bread for another use, if desired.

5. Brush ¼ cup Italian dressing evenly onto cut sides of bread. Arrange pepper strips in even layer in bottom half of loaf; top with even layer of onion. Brush onion with remaining 2 tablespoons Italian dressing; top with layer of basil and cheese. Replace bread top. Wrap loaf tightly in heavy-duty plastic wrap; refrigerate at least 2 hours or overnight.

6. When ready to serve, cut loaf crosswise into 1-inch slices. Secure with toothpicks and garnish, if desired.

Makes 12 servings

stuffed party baguette

chicken pesto pizza

1 loaf (1 pound) frozen bread dough, thawed

Nonstick cooking spray

8 ounces chicken tenders, cut into ½-inch pieces

½ red onion, cut into quarters and thinly sliced

¼ cup prepared pesto

2 large plum tomatoes, seeded and diced

1 cup (4 ounces) shredded pizza cheese blend or mozzarella cheese

Preheat oven to 375°F. Roll out bread dough on floured surface to 14×8-inch rectangle. Transfer to baking sheet sprinkled with cornmeal. Cover loosely with plastic wrap and let rise 20 to 30 minutes.

Meanwhile, spray large skillet with cooking spray; heat over medium heat. Add chicken; cook and stir 2 minutes. Add onion and pesto; cook and stir 3 to 4 minutes or until chicken is cooked through. Stir in tomatoes; remove from heat and let cool slightly.

Spread chicken mixture evenly over bread dough within 1 inch of edges. Sprinkle with cheese.

Bake on bottom rack of oven about 20 minutes or until crust is golden brown. Cut into 2-inch squares.

Makes about 20 appetizer pieces

italian artichoke dip

1 package (4 ounces) TREASURE CAVE® Shredded Italian Cheese Blend

1 package (8 ounces) cream cheese

½ cup mayonnaise

1 can (14 ounces) artichokes, drained and chopped

1 can (2¼ ounces) sliced ripe olives, drained

3 cloves garlic, minced

1. Remove cream cheese from wrapper. In a medium microwave safe bowl, heat cream cheese in 15-second intervals until softened.

2. Add remaining ingredients and stir until blended. Scrape mixture into a small baking dish.

3. Bake at 400°F for 25 minutes or until browned and bubbly. Serve warm with crackers.

Makes about 3 cups

chicken pesto pizza

spinach dip

1 cup sour cream

1 cup plain yogurt

4 HERB-OX® vegetable or beef bouillon granules

1 (10-ounce) package frozen spinach, thawed and well drained

½ cup shredded carrots

½ cup chopped water chestnuts

¼ cup minced green onion

1 small clove garlic, minced

Rye bread slices or cubes

Assorted fresh vegetables

In bowl, combine sour cream, yogurt and bouillon. Blend until bouillon is thoroughly dissolved. Add spinach, carrots, water chestnuts, green onion and garlic. Stir to blend. Cover and refrigerate several hours or overnight. Serve with Rye bread and fresh vegetables. *Makes about 3 cups*

Serving Suggestion: To serve dip, hollow out round loaf of Rye bread leaving a 1-inch border at the top. Fill bowl with spinach dip. Cut the remaining bread from the center of the loaf into pieces and serve with assorted fresh vegetables for dipping.

Prep Time: 15 minutes
Total Time: 3 to 24 hours

herbed-stuffed tomatoes

15 cherry tomatoes

½ cup low-fat (1%)
    cottage cheese

1 tablespoon thinly
    sliccd green onion

1 teaspoon chopped
    fresh chervil *or*
    ¼ teaspoon dried
    chcrvil leaves

½ teaspoon snipped
    fresh dill *or*
    ⅛ teaspoon dried
    dill weed

⅛ teaspoon lemon
    pepper

helpful hint

*Some recipes may not
offer both amounts of
fresh and dried herbs to
use. If fresh herbs are not
available, substitute 1
teaspoon of its dried
counterpart for 1
tablespoon of the
chopped fresh herb.*

Cut thin slice off bottom of each tomato. Scoop out
pulp with small spoon; discard pulp. Invert tomatoes
onto paper towels to drain.

Combine cottage cheese, green onion, chervil, dill and
lemon pepper in small bowl. Spoon into tomatoes.
Serve at once, or cover and refrigerate up to 8 hours.

Makes 5 servings

herbed-stuffed tomatoes

tortilla pizzettes

1 cup chunky salsa

1 cup refried beans

2 tablespoons chopped
fresh cilantro

½ teaspoon ground
cumin

3 large (10-inch) flour
tortillas

1 cup (4 ounces)
shredded Mexican
cheese blend

1. Pour salsa into strainer; let drain at least 20 minutes.

2. Meanwhile, combine refried beans, cilantro and cumin in small bowl; mix well. Preheat oven to 400°F. Spray baking sheet lightly with nonstick cooking spray; set aside.

3. Cut each tortilla into 2½-inch circles with round cookie cutter (9 to 10 circles per tortilla). Spread each tortilla circle with refried bean mixture, leaving ¼ inch around edge. Top each with heaping teaspoon drained salsa; sprinkle with about 1 teaspoon cheese.

4. Place pizzettes on prepared baking sheet. Bake about 7 minutes or until tortillas are golden brown.

Makes about 30 pizzettes

tortilla pizzettes

seasoned crab cakes

2 (6-ounce) cans crab meat, drained and chunked

2 eggs, beaten

½ cup dry bread crumbs

¼ cup minced green onion

¼ cup mayonnaise or salad dressing

1 tablespoon Dijon mustard

1 teaspoon Worcestershire sauce

2 teaspoons HERB-OX® Chicken Flavored Bouillon Granules, divided

½ cup crushed cornflake crumbs

Vegetable oil for frying

Lemon Wedges

Tarter sauce and Dijon style mustard

In bowl, combine first 7 ingredients and 1 teaspoon bouillon. Stir until combined. In another bowl, combine cornflake crumbs with remaining bouillon. Evenly divide crab mixture into 12 (2½-inch) patties. Coat patties with cornflake mixture. In large skillet, heat a small amount of oil. Place patties in skillet and cook over medium heat, about 3 minutes on each side, until golden brown. Add additional oil to skillet and continue cooking crab cakes. Serve immediately. If desired, garnish with lemon wedges and serve with tarter sauce and Dijon mustard. *Makes 12 servings*

Prep Time: 10 minutes
Total Time: 30 minutes

marinated chicken satay

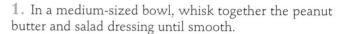

Marinade

2 tablespoons SMUCKER'S® Natural Peanut Butter

½ cup bottled Italian salad dressing

1 pound skinless, boneless chicken breast, cut into ½×4-inch strips

10-12 wooden skewers (soak in warm water for 30 minutes prior to use)

Dipping Sauce (recipe follows, optional)

1. In a medium-sized bowl, whisk together the peanut butter and salad dressing until smooth.

2. Place chicken strips in peanut butter mixture. Marinate in covered bowl 3 hours or overnight in refrigerator.

3. Heat broiler on high. Remove chicken from refrigerator. Thread 2 chicken strips onto each skewer.

4. Arrange skewers on a metal grill rack positioned over a foil-lined baking pan. Broil skewers 6 minutes; turn skewers over. Broil another 4-6 minutes, or until juices run clear and chicken is thoroughly cooked.*

5. Serve chicken skewers with dipping sauce, if desired. *Makes 3 to 4 servings*

*To grill, place skewered chicken on hot grill for 8 minutes or until juices run clear

dipping sauce

½ cup SMUCKER'S® Natural Peanut Butter

6 tablespoons water

½ cup chopped parsley or cilantro leaves

3 tablespoons fresh lime juice

2 tablespoons reduced-sodium soy sauce

1 tablespoon honey

1 teaspoon sesame oil

Pinch cayenne pepper

Place all ingredients in a blender; blend on medium-high until smooth.

MEAT FACTS

Don't be terrified of not having enough ideas for what to make for lunch or dinner. There are so many great meal ideas when it comes to cooking beef and pork. Beginning cooks often find cooking beef and pork baffling because there are so many different cuts. The recipes in this chapter feature some of the easiest cuts of meat to prepare. Try Quick Beef Stroganoff (page 61) or Stuffed Apricot Pork Chops (page 69). Both these recipes and so many on the following pages are simple to prepare as well as delicious!

Read the following pages to discover the variety that beef and pork offers. You'll also learn about purchasing and storing meat, cooking methods and how to determine doneness. Also, you'll find helpful tips for using your slow cooker and discover how easy it is to cook tasty meals. You'll be cooking meat like a gourmet chef in no time!

BUYING FRESH MEAT

In order to ensure that you are buying the freshest meat possible, look for packages that are securely wrapped with no signs of leakage, excess liquid or tears. The meat also should be cold to the touch. Choose fresh meat that has good color. Avoid meat that is pale or gray-colored. Any fat should be firm and creamy white, not yellow. The meat should have no odd odors. The surface should be moist but not slimy. Always check the "sell-by" date and purchase on or before that date. Meat should only be purchased from a refrigerated case and should be securely wrapped and transported home quickly for immediate refrigeration. In addition, look for cuts of meat that are uniform in size so that they will cook evenly.

Beef: When choosing beef, look for: 1) marbling or flecks and thin streaks of fat that run throughout the piece of beef, 2) a bright, cherry-red color (avoid meat with a grayish tone or yellow fat), 3) beef that is firm to the touch and 4) the cut. Cuts marked "loin" or "rib" tend to be more tender, while chuck, round and flank tend to be less tender.

MEAT FACTS

Pork: When choosing pork, look for: 1) moist meat that is pink in color (avoid meat with dry or discolored surfaces or a reddish or gray color), 2) fat that is milky white and 3) the cut. Cuts marked "loin" or "leg" tend to be leaner. Lean cuts include tenderloin, loin chop and sirloin roast. (Check labels for cured or smoked pork cuts such as hams or sausages to see if the meat is "fully-cooked" or if it needs to be "cooked-before-eating.")

TESTING FOR DONENESS
Use these guidelines below to determine the doneness of meat.

Type of Meat		Temperature
Beef (all cuts but ground)		
	Medium-Rare	145°F
	Medium	160°F
	Well-Done	170°F
Ground Beef		
	Medium	160°F
Pork and Veal		
	Medium	160°F
	Well-Done	170°F
Ham		
	Fully-Cooked Ham	140°F
	Uncooked Ham	170°F
Lamb		
	Medium-Rare	145°F
	Medium	160°F
	Well-Done	170°F

MEAT FACTS

STORAGE AND HANDLING

•Meat is very susceptible to contamination and spoilage so care should be taken in handling and storage to maintain quality and food safety. After working with fresh meat, either to prepare for storage or for cooking, always wash your hands and all utensils and surfaces that have been in contact with the meat before continuing another task.

•Meat may be stored in its original supermarket wrap unless the package is leaking. Store fresh meat in the coldest part of the refrigerator, about 36° to 40°F and use within two to three days. If not used within this time, wrap in moisture-proof material, label, date and freeze at 0°F or lower. After cooking, meat may be refrigerated three days or frozen for three months.

•Thaw meat, still wrapped, in the refrigerator about four to seven hours per pound, usually overnight. Once meat is thawed completely, it should be used within a day or two and not refrozen. Meat can also be thawed in a microwave oven. Follow the microwave oven manufacturer's directions for thawing, being careful not to begin cooking the edges of the meat. Use meat that has been thawed in the microwave immediately.

COMMON CUTS AND COOKING METHODS

A good rule of thumb for determining whether a cut of fresh meat is tough or tender is the original location of the cut on the carcass. Less tender cuts come from the shoulder, leg and rump muscles of the animal because these muscles are used more. The muscles of the midsection of the animal provide more tender cuts.

Dry-Heat Cooking Methods: These are good methods for cooking tender cuts of meat or tough cuts that have been tenderized. Broiling, grilling, panbroiling, panfrying roasting and stir-frying are all examples of dry-heat cooking.

Moist-Heat Cooking Methods: Braising; simmering or stewing are all examples of moist-heat cooking. They are appropriate methods for cooking tough cuts. The moisture tenderizes the connective tissue between the muscle fibers.

SLOW COOKING

The slow cooker is a very effortless way to cook. Start by placing meats and vegetables into the slow cooker. Then set it to the correct temperature; set the timer and wait for a delicious meal to be complete. There is only one dish to clean-up and there is extra time to do so many other things.

The Benefits

•No need for constant attention or frequent stirring

•No worry about burning or overcooking

•No sink full of pots and pans to scrub at the end of a long day

•Great for parties and buffets

•The kitchen stays cool because the oven is not turned on

•Saves energy—cooking on the low setting uses less energy than most light bulbs

Keep a Lid On It: A slow cooker can take as long as twenty minutes to regain heat lost when the cover is removed. If the recipe calls for stirring or checking the dish near the end of the cooking time, replace the cover as quickly as possible. Otherwise, resist the urge to remove the cover.

Cleaning Your Slow Cooker: To clean the slow cooker, follow the manufacturer's instructions. To make cleanup even easier, spray with nonstick cooking spray before adding food.

Selecting the Right Meat: A good tip to keep in mind is that tougher, inexpensive cuts of meat should be used in the slow cooker. Top-quality cuts, such as loin chops or filet mignon, fall apart during long cooking periods and therefore are not good choices to use in the slow cooker. Keep those cuts for roasting, broiling or grilling, and save money when using the slow cooker.

INVITING BEEF & PORK

beef in wine sauce

4 pounds boneless beef chuck roast, cut into 1½- to 2-inch cubes

2 tablespoons garlic powder

2 cans (10¾ ounces each) condensed golden mushroom soup, undiluted

1 can (8 ounces) sliced mushrooms, drained

¾ cup dry sherry

1 envelope (about 1 ounce) dry onion soup mix

1 bag (20 ounces) frozen sliced carrots, thawed

1. Preheat oven to 325°F. Spray heavy 4-quart casserole or Dutch oven with nonstick cooking spray.

2. Sprinkle beef with garlic powder. Place in prepared casserole.

3. Combine canned soup, mushrooms, sherry and dry soup mix in medium bowl. Pour over meat; mix well.

4. Cover; bake 3 hours or until meat is very tender. Add carrots during last 15 minutes of baking.

Makes 6 to 8 servings

beef in wine sauce

apricot pork chops and dressing

1 box (6 ounces) herb-seasoned stuffing mix

½ cup dried apricots (about 16), cut into quarters

6 sheets (18×12-inches) heavy-duty foil, lightly sprayed with nonstick cooking spray

6 bone-in pork chops, ½ inch thick

Salt

Black pepper

6 tablespoons apricot jam

1 bag (16 ounces) frozen green peas

3 cups matchstick carrots*

*Precut matchstick carrots are available in the produce section of large supermarkets.

1. Preheat oven to 450°F. Prepare stuffing mix according to package directions; stir in apricots.

2. Place ½ cup stuffing mixture in center of one sheet of foil. Place 1 pork chop over stuffing mixture, pressing down slightly and shaping stuffing to conform to shape of chop. Sprinkle chop with salt and pepper. Spread 1 tablespoon apricot jam over pork chop.

3. Place ⅔ cup peas beside pork chop in curve of bone. Arrange ½ cup carrots around outside of chop.

4. Double fold sides and ends of foil to seal packet, leaving head space for heat circulation. Repeat with remaining stuffing mixture, pork chops, salt, pepper, jam and vegetables to make 5 more packets. Place packets on baking sheet.

5. Bake 25 minutes or until pork chops are barely pink in centers and vegetables are tender. Remove from oven. Carefully open one end of each packet to allow steam to escape. Open packets and transfer contents to serving plates. *Makes 6 servings*

helpful hint

Preparing single-serve foil meal packets and freezing them for later use makes meal preparation a breeze. When you don't feel like preparing a meal for one or someone needs to eat early, just pull a packet out of the freezer, pop it into the oven and relax until dinner is ready.

apricot pork chop and dressing

chipotle taco filling

2 pounds ground beef chuck

2 cups chopped yellow onion

2 cans (15 ounces each) pinto beans, rinsed and drained

1 can (14½ ounces) diced tomatoes with peppers and onions, drained

4 chipotle peppers in adobo sauce, mashed

1 tablespoon beef bouillon granules

1 tablespoon sugar

1½ teaspoons ground cumin

Slow Cooker Directions

Place a medium skillet over medium-high heat until hot. Add beef and cook 6 minutes or until just beginning to brown, stirring frequently. Place beef and accumulated juices and remaining ingredients into slow cooker. Cover and cook on LOW 4 hours or on HIGH 2 hours. Serve in taco shells or flour tortillas, with shredded lettuce, salsa, shredded cheese and sour cream, if desired. *Makes 8 cups, enough for 16 tacos*

chipotle taco filling

asian ginger glazed pork

1 pound pork tenderloin

2 tablespoons
    cornstarch

4 green onions with
    tops

1 piece fresh ginger
    (1 inch long), peeled

3 tablespoons vegetable
    oil, divided

2 cloves garlic, minced

¼ cup dry sherry

1 tablespoon soy sauce

1 to 2 tablespoons
    water

2 teaspoons light brown
    sugar

¼ teaspoon red pepper
    flakes

¼ cup unsalted roasted
    cashews, chopped

Hot cooked rice

Fresh herb sprigs and
    bell pepper triangles
    for garnish

Trim fat from pork; discard. Cut pork crosswise into ¼-inch-thick slices. Place cornstarch on waxed paper. Coat both sides of pork with cornstarch. Reserve remaining cornstarch. Set aside.

Cut onions into 1-inch pieces. Thinly slice ginger. Stack ginger, a few slices at a time, and cut into fine strips. Set aside.

Heat wok over high heat about 1 minute or until hot. Drizzle 1 tablespoon oil into wok and heat 30 seconds. Add half of pork; stir-fry until well browned on both sides. Remove pork to plate. Repeat with 1 tablespoon oil and remaining pork. Reduce heat to medium.

Add remaining 1 tablespoon oil to wok and heat 30 seconds. Add ginger, garlic and onions to wok; stir-fry 1 minute. Stir in reserved cornstarch. Add sherry, soy sauce, 1 tablespoon water, brown sugar and red pepper. Cook and stir until sauce boils and thickens. Stir in additional water if needed.

Spoon sauce over pork until coated and glazed. Sprinkle with cashews. Serve with rice. Garnish, if desired.

Makes 4 servings

Note: Cashews, kidney-shaped nuts with a sweet buttery flavor, add a nice crunch to this dish.

southwest bean chili

1 can (16 ounces)
   tomato sauce

2 medium green bell
   peppers, seeded and
   chopped

1 can (15 ounces)
   garbanzo beans,
   rinsed and drained

1 can (15 ounces) red
   kidney beans, rinsed
   and drained

1 can (15 ounces) black
   beans, rinsed and
   drained

1 can (14½ ounces)
   Mexican-style
   stewed tomatoes,
   undrained

1½ cups frozen corn

1 cup chicken broth

3 tablespoons chili
   powder

4 cloves garlic, minced

1 tablespoon
   unsweetened cocoa
   powder

1 teaspoon ground
   cumin

½ teaspoon salt

   Hot cooked rice

Slow Cooker Directions
Combine all ingredients except rice and toppings in slow cooker; stir until well blended. Cover and cook on LOW 6 to 6½ hours or until vegetables are tender.

Spoon rice into bowls; top with chili. Serve with toppings, if desired.   *Makes 8 to 10 servings*

helpful hint

Top chili with shredded cheese, sliced ripe olives, avocado and green onion slices, if desired.

italian pork chops

**2 cups uncooked long-
grain white rice**

**4 large pork chops
(½ inch thick)**

**1 teaspoon basil,
crushed**

**1 can (26 ounces) DEL
MONTE® Spaghetti
Sauce with
Mushrooms or
Chunky Italian Herb
Spaghetti Sauce**

**1 green bell pepper, cut
into thin strips**

helpful hint

*Serve pork chops with
baked potatoes and
vegetables.*

1. Cook rice according to package directions.

2. Preheat broiler. Sprinkle meat with basil; season with salt and black pepper, if desired. Place meat on broiler pan. Broil 4 inches from heat about 6 minutes on each side or until no longer pink in center.

3. Combine sauce and green pepper in microwaveable dish. Cover with plastic wrap; slit to vent. Microwave on HIGH 5 to 6 minutes or until green pepper is tender-crisp and sauce is heated through. Add meat; cover with sauce. Microwave 1 minute. Serve over hot rice.

Makes 4 servings

italian pork chops

mexican meatloaf

2 pounds ground beef

2 cups crushed corn chips

1 cup shredded Cheddar cheese

⅔ cup salsa

2 eggs, beaten

4 tablespoons taco seasoning

Slow Cooker Directions

1. Combine all ingredients in large bowl; mix well.

2. Shape meat mixture into loaf and place in slow cooker. Cover; cook on LOW 8 to 10 hours.

Makes 4 to 6 servings

Tip: For a glaze, mix together ½ cup ketchup, 2 tablespoons brown sugar and 1 teaspoon dry mustard. Spread over meatloaf. Cover; cook on HIGH 15 minutes.

easy moo shu pork

7 ounces pork tenderloin

Nonstick olive oil cooking spray

4 green onions, cut into ½-inch pieces

2 tablespoons hoisin sauce or Asian plum sauce

1½ cups packaged cole slaw mix

4 (8-inch) fat-free flour tortillas, warmed

1. Thinly slice pork. Lightly spray large nonstick skillet with cooking spray. Heat over medium-high heat. Add pork and green onions; stir-fry 2 to 3 minutes or until pork is no longer pink. Stir in hoisin sauce and cole slaw mix.

2. Spoon pork mixture onto tortillas. Wrap to enclose. Serve immediately. *Makes 2 servings*

Note: To warm tortillas, stack and wrap loosely in plastic wrap. Microwave on HIGH for 15 to 20 seconds or until hot and pliable.

mexican meatloaf

slow cooker pizza casserole

1½ pounds ground beef, cooked and drained

1 pound sausage, cooked and drained

1 pound corkscrew pasta, cooked and drained

4 jars (14 ounces each) pizza sauce

2 cups (8 ounces) shredded mozzarella cheese

2 cups freshly grated Parmesan cheese

2 cans (4 ounces each) mushroom stems and pieces, drained

2 packages (3 ounces each) sliced pepperoni

½ cup finely chopped onion

½ cup finely chopped green pepper

1 clove garlic minced

Slow Cooker Directions

1. Combine all ingredients in slow cooker.

2. Cover; cook on LOW 4 hours or HIGH 2 hours.

Makes 6 servings

slow cooker pizza casserole

stir-fried cajun pork

1 pound boneless pork
loin, cut into
julienne strips

4 tablespoons Cajun-
Style Seasoning
(recipe follows)

1 red bell pepper, diced

1 tart green apple, cored
and diced

¼ cup pecan pieces

1 teaspoon vegetable oil

Season pork strips with 2 tablespoons Cajun-Style Seasoning. Toss pepper, apple and pecans with 2 tablespoons seasoning; reserve.

Heat oil in nonstick skillet over medium-high heat. Stir-fry pork 2 minutes; add reserved pepper mixture. Cook and stir 2 minutes. Serve immediately.

Makes 4 servings

Prep Time: 10 minutes
Cook Time: 10 minutes

cajun-style seasoning

3 tablespoons paprika

1 tablespoon garlic powder

2 teaspoons dried oregano leaves

2 teaspoons dried thyme leaves

½ teaspoon salt

½ teaspoon white pepper

½ teaspoon ground cumin

½ teaspoon cayenne pepper

¼ teaspoon ground nutmeg

Combine all ingredients in small bowl; mix well.

Makes ½ cup

*Favorite recipe from **National Pork Board***

spicy beefy noodles

1½ pounds ground beef

1 small onion, minced

1 small clove garlic, minced

1 tablespoon chili powder

1 teaspoon paprika

⅛ teaspoon *each* dried basil leaves, dill weed, dried thyme leaves and dried marjoram leaves

Salt

Black pepper

1 can (10 ounces) diced tomatoes with green chilies, undrained

1 can (8 ounces) tomato sauce

1 cup water

3 tablespoons Worcestershire sauce

1 package (about 10 ounces) egg noodles, cooked according to package directions

½ cup (2 ounces) *each* shredded Cheddar, mozzarella, Pepper-Jack and provolone cheeses

1. Cook and stir ground beef, onion and garlic in large skillet over medium heat until meat is no longer pink, stirring to separate meat. Pour off drippings. Add chili powder, paprika, basil, dill, thyme and marjoram. Season with salt and pepper. Cook and stir 2 minutes.

2. Add tomatoes with juice, tomato sauce, water and Worcestershire sauce; mix well. Simmer, covered, 20 minutes.

3. In 2-quart microwavable casserole, combine meat mixture and noodles. Mix cheeses and sprinkle evenly over top.

4. Microwave at HIGH 3 minutes. Let stand 5 minutes. Microwave 3 minutes longer or until cheeses melt.

Makes 6 servings

spicy beefy noodles

bbq shortribs with cola sauce

1 large (17×15 inches) foil bag

1 can (12 ounces) regular cola

1 can (6 ounces) tomato paste

¾ cup honey

½ cup cider vinegar

1 teaspoon salt

2 cloves garlic, minced

Dash hot pepper sauce (optional)

4 pounds beef shortribs, cut into 2-inch lengths

1. Preheat oven to 450°F. Place foil bag in 1-inch deep jelly-roll pan. Spray inside of bag with nonstick cooking spray. Dust with flour.

2. To prepare sauce, combine cola, tomato paste, honey, vinegar, salt, garlic and hot pepper sauce, if desired, in 2-quart saucepan. Bring to a boil over medium-high heat. Reduce heat slightly and cook, stirring occasionally, until slightly reduced, about 15 minutes.

3. Dip each shortrib in sauce. Place ribs in single layer in prepared foil bag. Ladle additional 1 cup sauce into bag. Seal bag, leaving headspace for heat circulation by folding open end twice.

4. Bake 1 hour 15 minutes or until ribs are cooked through. Carefully cut open bag.

Makes 4 to 6 servings

bbq shortribs with cola sauce

cheese-stuffed meat loaves

⅓ cup fine dry bread crumbs

2 ounces Cheddar cheese, cut into four 3×½×½-inch pieces

¾ cup ketchup

1 tablespoon all-purpose flour

1 tablespoon prepared mustard

1 egg, lightly beaten

¼ cup sliced green onions

½ teaspoon salt

¼ teaspoon black pepper

1 pound lean ground beef

1 large (17×15 inches) foil bag

2 tablespoons dill pickle relish

1. Preheat oven to 450°F. Place 1 tablespoon of bread crumbs on sheet of wax paper. Set remaining bread crumbs aside. Roll cheese pieces in bread crumbs, pressing crumbs onto all sides. Set aside.

2. Combine ketchup, flour and mustard in small bowl. Set aside.

3. Combine egg, remaining bread crumbs, onions, 3 tablespoons ketchup mixture, salt and pepper in large bowl. Add ground beef; mix well. Form meat mixture into four individual (3½×2×1½-inch) meat loaves, shaping each loaf around piece of cheese. Completely enclose cheese with meat mixture.

4. Place foil bag in shallow baking pan. Spread half remaining ketchup mixture on center of one side of foil bag. Place meat loaves on top of ketchup mixture, leaving about 1-inch space between loaves. Spread remaining ketchup mixture over top of loaves.

5. Double fold open side of bag, leaving head space for heat circulation. Bake 25 to 30 minutes or until internal temperature reaches 170°F. Carefully open bag and transfer meatloaves to serving plates. Sprinkle pickle relish on top of each meat loaf. *Makes 4 servings*

szechuan pork & vegetables

4 butterflied pork loin chops, ½ inch thick (1 to 1¼ pounds)

¼ cup plus 1 tablespoon stir-fry sauce, divided

¾ teaspoon bottled minced ginger *or* **½ teaspoon ground ginger**

1 package (16 ounces) frozen Asian-style vegetables, thawed

1 can (5 ounces) crisp chow mein noodles

2 tablespoons chopped green onion

1. Heat large, deep nonstick skillet over medium heat until hot. Add pork. Spoon 1 tablespoon stir-fry sauce over pork; sprinkle with ginger. Cook 3 minutes. Turn pork; cook 3 minutes. Transfer chops to plate; set aside.

2. Add vegetables and remaining ¼ cup stir-fry sauce to skillet. Cook over medium-low heat 3 minutes; add pork. Cook 3 minutes or until pork is barely pink in center, stirring vegetables and turning chops once.

3. While pork is cooking, arrange chow mein noodles around edges of 4 serving plates. Transfer chops to plates. Top noodles with vegetable mixture. Sprinkle with green onion.

Makes 4 servings

Prep and Cook Time: 12 minutes

helpful hint

Usually the butcher can butterfly the pork chops for you. If you prefer to do it yourself, follow these instructions: Cut horizontally through the thickest portions, stopping about 1 inch from the opposite edge so that the meat can open like a book. Trim any fat, if desired.

szechuan pork & vegetables

easy homemade barbecue

Water

1 boneless pork blade
   (butt) roast
   (3 to 4 pounds)

Salt

Black pepper

1 bottle (16 ounces)
   barbecue sauce

Hamburger buns or
   sandwich rolls

*Depending on the size of
your roast, you may not
need to use an entire
bottle of barbecue sauce.
This recipe is equally
tasty when made with
other cuts of pork roast.*

Slow Cooker Directions

1. Cover bottom of slow cooker with 2 inches of water. Place roast in slow cooker; season with salt and pepper to taste. Cover and cook on LOW 8 to 10 hours.

2. Remove roast from slow cooker; let stand 15 minutes. Discard liquid remaining in slow cooker. Using 2 forks, shred cooked roast. Return meat to slow cooker. Add barbecue sauce; mix well. Cover and cook on HIGH 30 minutes. To serve, spoon barbecue mixture onto buns.   *Makes 8 to 10 servings*

easy homemade barbecue

quick beef stroganoff

1½ pounds lean ½-inch-thick top sirloin steak, cut into 2-inch strips

3 cups sliced fresh mushrooms

1 can (10½ ounces) condensed beef broth

3 tablespoons all-purpose flour

5 teaspoons MRS. DASH® Onion & Herb Blend

½ cup fat-free sour cream

4 cups cooked wide egg noodles

Vegetable cooking spray

Paprika

Fresh parsley

Spray large skillet with vegetable cooking spray. Sauté steak 5 minutes, or until no longer pink. Add mushrooms and continue cooking for 1 minute. Combine beef broth, flour and Onion & Herb Blend; mix well. Add to meat and mushrooms. Bring to a boil stirring frequently; continue stirring 1 minute. Just before serving, stir in sour cream. Serve over egg noodles. Sprinkle with paprika and garnish with parsley.

Makes 8 servings

Preparation Time: 10 minutes
Cooking Time: 10 minutes

helpful hint

Do not peel mushrooms. Also, do not wash mushrooms until you are ready to use them. To wash mushrooms, wipe them clean with a damp paper towel—do no soak them in water. Cut off a small slice from the bottom of each mushroom and they are ready to use.

dijon baby back ribs

4 pounds baby back pork ribs

1 bottle (12 ounces) LAWRY'S® Dijon & Honey Marinade With Lemon Juice, divided

If needed, cut ribs in lengths to fit in large resealable plastic bag. Place ribs in bag and add ¾ cup Dijon & Honey Marinade; seal bag and shake to coat. Marinate in refrigerator overnight. Remove ribs form bag, discarding used marinade. Place ribs on broiler pan that has been sprayed with nonstick cooking spray. Bake in 300°F oven until tender; no longer pink, about 2 hours. Finish on grill, brushing often with remaining Marinade, until glazed.   *Makes 4 servings*

Meal Idea: Serve with corn on the cob, coleslaw and baked beans for a real barbecue treat.

Variation: Ribs may be cut into individual ribs after grilling and served as appetizers or 'finger food'. Great for parties!

Prep. Time: 5 minutes
Marinate Time: Overnight
Cook Time: 2 hours 10 minutes

dijon baby back ribs

pork chops with balsamic vinegar

2 boneless center pork loin chops, 1½ inch thick

1½ teaspoons lemon pepper

1 teaspoon vegetable oil

3 tablespoons balsamic vinegar

2 tablespoons chicken broth

2 teaspoons butter

Pat chops dry. Coat with lemon pepper. Heat oil in heavy skillet over medium-high heat. Add chops. Brown on first side 8 minutes; turn and cook 7 minutes more or until no longer pink in center. Remove from pan and keep warm. Add vinegar and broth to skillet; cook, stirring, until syrupy (about 1 to 2 minutes). Stir in butter until blended. Spoon sauce over chops.

Makes 2 servings

Prep Time: 20 minutes

*Favorite recipe from **National Pork Board***

pork chop with balsamic vinegar

fajita-style beef wraps

½ **pound top sirloin**
   steak

1 **package (1.27 ounces)**
   LAWRY'S® Fajita
   Spices & Seasonings

2 **tablespoons vegetable**
   oil

½ **cup chopped green**
   bell pepper

1 **cup thinly sliced red**
   onion

1 **can (8¾ ounces)**
   garbanzo beans,
   drained

1 **tomato, quartered and**
   thinly sliced

8 **large (burrito size)** *or*
   12 small (soft taco
   size) flour tortillas,
   warmed to soften

In small bowl, mix together Fajita Spices & Seasonings and oil. Spread 1 teaspoon of seasoning paste evenly over each side of steak. Set aside remaining seasoning paste. Grill or broil meat to desired doneness. Slice into thin strips. If a more intense flavor is desired, cover and refrigerate steak 30 minutes before grilling or broiling. In large bowl, combine green pepper, onion, garbanzo beans, tomato, steak and remaining seasoning paste; stir to coat evenly. Scoop ½ or ⅓ cup beef mixture on each tortilla. Fold in sides and roll-up to enclose filling. Wrap each burrito in plastic wrap and refrigerate until ready to serve or transport to picnic.

Makes 8 large or 12 small wraps

Hint: Filling may be prepared the night before then wrapped in tortillas the next day or at the picnic!

Prep. Time: 10 to 15 minutes
Cook Time: 8 to 10 minutes

fajita-style beef wraps

simple shredded pork tacos

2 pounds boneless pork roast

1 cup salsa

1 can (4 ounces) chopped green chilies

½ teaspoon garlic salt

½ teaspoon pepper

Slow Cooker Directions

1. Place all ingredients in slow cooker.

2. Cover; cook on LOW 8 hours, or until meat is tender. To serve, use 2 forks to shred pork.

Makes 6 servings

Serving Suggestion: Serve with tortillas and your favorite condiments.

jambalaya

1 pound ground beef

1 cup chopped onion

¼ cup diced green bell pepper

1 can (28 ounces) tomatoes, liquid drained and reserved

1 teaspoon salt

½ teaspoon sugar

¼ teaspoon dried thyme leaves

1 small bay leaf

2⅓ cups cooked rice

1. Heat large skillet over medium heat. Add beef, onion and bell pepper; cook and stir until meat is no longer pink. Drain fat.

2. Add enough water to reserved tomato liquid to make 1½ cups. Add liquid, tomatoes, salt, sugar, thyme and bay leaf to skillet. Simmer 5 minutes.

3. Stir in rice; cover and simmer 5 minutes longer. Remove and discard bay leaf before serving.

Makes 4 to 6 servings

simple shredded pork tacos

ginger beef and pineapple kabobs

1 cup LAWRY'S® Thai Ginger Marinade With Lime Juice, divided

1 can (16 ounces) pineapple chunks, juice reserved

1½ pounds boneless beef top sirloin steak, cut into 1½-inch cubes

2 red bell peppers, cut into chunks

2 medium onions, cut into wedges

In large resealable plastic food storage bag, combine ½ cup Thai Ginger Marinade and 1 tablespoon pineapple juice; mix well. Add steak, bell peppers and onions; seal bag. Marinate in refrigerator at least 30 minutes. Remove steak and vegetables; discard used marinade. Alternately thread steak, vegetables and pineapple onto skewers. Grill or broil skewers 10 to 15 minutes or until desired doneness, turning once and basting often with additional ½ cup Thai Ginger Marinade. Do not baste during last 5 minutes of cooking. Discard any remaining marinade.

Makes 6 servings

Serving Suggestion: Serve kabobs with a light salad and bread.

ginger beef and pineapple kabobs

stuffed apricot pork chops

¾ **cup seasoned stuffing mix**

¾ **cup chopped dried apricots**

2 **tablespoons chopped red onion**

2 **tablespoons slivered almonds**

2 **tablespoons chicken broth**

4 **(1-inch thick) center-cut pork chops**

Salt and pepper

1 **teaspoon paprika**

4 **sheets (18×12 inches) heavy-duty foil, lightly sprayed with nonstick cooking spray**

¼ **cup apricot preserves**

1 **teaspoon Dijon-style mustard**

1 **teaspoon soy sauce**

1. Preheat oven to 450°F. Combine stuffing mix, apricots, onion, almonds and broth in medium bowl.

2. Place pork chops on cutting board, cut horizontal pocket in each chop. Season cut surfaces with salt and pepper. Place stuffing mixture in pork chops. Rub both sides of pork chop with paprika. Place each pork chop on foil sheet.

3. Combine apricot preserves, mustard and soy sauce in small bowl. Spoon about 1 tablespoon preserve mixture on top of each chop. Double fold sides and ends of foil to seal packet, leaving head space for heat circulation. Place packets on baking sheet.

4. Bake 20 to 23 minutes or until pork is cooked through. *Makes 4 servings*

helpful hint

Cooking in foil is a convenient way to save time. There is minimal preparation and clean-up is so simple.

beef teriyaki stir-fry

1 cup uncooked rice

1 boneless beef top sirloin steak (about 1 pound)

½ cup teriyaki marinade, divided

2 tablespoons vegetable oil, divided

1 medium onion, halved and sliced

2 cups frozen green beans, rinsed and drained

1. Cook rice according to package directions, omitting salt.

2. Cut beef lengthwise in half, then crosswise into ⅛-inch slices. Combine beef and ¼ cup marinade in medium bowl; set aside.

3. Heat 1½ teaspoons oil in wok or large skillet over medium-high heat until hot. Add onion; stir-fry 3 to 4 minutes or until crisp-tender. Remove from wok to medium bowl.

4. Heat 1½ teaspoons oil in wok. Stir-fry beans 3 minutes or until crisp-tender and hot. Drain off excess liquid. Add beans to onions in bowl.

5. Heat remaining 1 tablespoon oil in wok. Drain beef, discarding marinade. Stir-fry half of beef 2 minutes or until barely pink in center. Remove to bowl. Repeat with remaining beef. Return beef and accumulated juices in bowl to wok. Stir in vegetables and remaining ¼ cup marinade; cook and stir 1 minute or until heated through. Serve with rice. *Makes 4 servings*

Prep and Cook Time: 22 minutes

beef teriyaki stir-fry

grilled honey garlic pork chops

¼ **cup lemon juice**

¼ **cup honey**

2 **tablespoons soy sauce**

1 **tablespoon dry sherry**

2 **cloves garlic, minced**

4 **boneless center-cut lean pork chops (about 4 ounces each)**

Combine all ingredients except pork chops in small bowl. Place pork in shallow baking dish; pour marinade over pork. Cover and refrigerate 4 hours or overnight. Remove pork from marinade. Heat remaining marinade in small saucepan over medium heat to a simmer. Grill pork over medium-hot coals 12 to 15 minutes, turning once during cooking and basting frequently with marinade, until meat thermometer registers 155° to 160°F. *Makes 4 servings*

Favorite recipe from **National Honey Board**

broccoli beef

2 **tablespoons vegetable oil**

1 **teaspoon chopped shallots**

10 **ounces sliced boneless beef**

6 **tablespoons LEE KUM KEE® Stir-Fry Sauce, LEE KUM KEE® Spicy Stir-Fry Sauce or LEE KUM KEE® Stir-Fry Sauce Kung Pao, divided**

1 **cup cooked broccoli florets**

Heat skillet over medium heat. Add oil. Sauté shallots. Add beef and 2 tablespoons Stir-Fry Sauce; stir-fry. When beef is half done, add broccoli and remaining 4 tablespoons Stir-Fry Sauce. Cook and stir until beef is done and broccoli is tender and heated through.

Makes 4 servings

grilled honey garlic pork chop

southwest steak

¾ cup Italian dressing

½ cup minced fresh parsley

⅓ cup *Frank's® RedHot®* Original Cayenne Pepper Sauce

3 tablespoons lime juice

1 tablespoon *French's®* Worcestershire Sauce

2 pounds boneless sirloin or top round steak (1½ inches thick)

1. Place dressing, parsley, **Frank's RedHot** Sauce, lime juice and Worcestershire in blender or food processor. Cover; process until smooth. Reserve ⅔ cup sauce. Pour remaining sauce over steak in deep dish. Cover; refrigerate 30 minutes.

2. Grill or broil steak 8 minutes per side for medium-rare or to desired doneness. Let stand 5 minutes. Slice steak and serve with reserved sauce.

Makes 6 to 8 servings

Prep Time: 10 minutes
Marinate Time: 30 minutes
Cook Time: 20 minutes

southwest steak

thai beef stir fry

2 packages UNCLE
  BEN'S NATURAL
  SELECT® Garlic &
  Butter Rice

1 pound sirloin beef, cut
  into strips and
  seasoned with salt
  and pepper

16 ounces package frozen
  Oriental
  vegetables,* thawed
  and drained

2 tablespoons oil

1 can bamboo shoots,
  drained

14 ounces can coconut
  milk

2 tablespoons soy sauce

2 tablespoons hot sauce
  or to taste

2 limes, juice only

12 lime slices for garnish

6 Thai chili peppers for
  garnish

1. Cook rice according to package directions.

2. In skillet, heat oil and brown beef; add vegetables and bamboo shoots. Sauté 1 minute; drain excess liquid. Add coconut milk, soy sauce, hot sauce, and lime juice; simmer until sauce thickens.

3. Serve over rice, garnish with 2 lime slices and 1 Thai chili pepper.   *Makes 6 servings*

Preparation Time: 25 minutes

helpful hint

You may substitute ½ cup each of your favorite fresh vegetables such as red and yellow peppers, sugar snap peas and broccoli for the frozen Oriental vegetables. Sauté with beef for 2 minutes.

rosemary garlic rub

2 tablespoons chopped
fresh rosemary

1½ teaspoons LAWRY'S®
Seasoned Salt

1 teaspoon LAWRY'S®
Garlic Pepper

½ teaspoon LAWRY'S®
Garlic Powder with
Parsley

1 pound beef top sirloin
steak

1 tablespoon olive oil

In small bowl, combine rosemary, Seasoned Salt, Garlic Pepper and Garlic Powder with Parsley; mix well. Brush both sides of steak with oil. Sprinkle with herb mixture, pressing onto steak. Grill or broil steak 15 to 20 minutes or until desired doneness, turning halfway through grilling time. *Makes 4 servings*

Meal Idea: Serve with oven roasted or French fried potatoes and honey-coated carrots.

Hint: This rub is also great on lamb or pork.

Prep. Time: 2 minutes
Cook Time: 15 to 20 minutes

rosemary garlic rub

angel hair carbonara

⅔ cup milk

2 tablespoons margarine or butter

1 package (4.8 ounces) PASTA RONI® Angel Hair Pasta with Herbs

2 cups chopped cooked pork or ham

1 package (10 ounces) frozen peas

¼ cup sliced green onions

1. In round 3-quart microwavable glass casserole, combine 1½ cups water, milk and margarine. Microwave, uncovered, on HIGH 4 to 5 minutes or until boiling.

2. Gradually add pasta while stirring. Separate pasta with fork, if needed.

3. Stir in Special Seasonings.

4. Microwave, uncovered, on HIGH 4 minutes, stirring gently after 2 minutes. Separate pasta with fork, if needed. Stir in pork, frozen peas and onions. Continue to microwave 2 to 3 minutes. Sauce will be thin, but will thicken upon standing.

5. Let stand 3 minutes or until desired consistency. Stir before serving. *Makes 4 servings*

maple-mustard pork chops

2 tablespoons maple syrup, divided

1 tablespoon olive oil

2 teaspoons whole-grain mustard

2 center-cut pork loin chops (6 ounces each)

Nonstick cooking spray

⅓ cup water

1. Preheat oven to 375°F. Combine maple syrup, olive oil and mustard in small bowl. Brush syrup mixture over both sides of pork chops.

2. Spray medium ovenproof skillet with cooking spray; heat it over medium-high heat. Add chops; brown on both sides. Add water; cover and bake 20 to 30 minutes or until barely pink in center. *Makes 2 servings*

glazed pork loin

1 bag (1 pound) baby carrots

4 boneless pork loin chops

1 jar (8 ounces) apricot preserves

helpful hint

Serve this dish with seasoned or cheese-flavored instant mashed potatoes.

Slow Cooker Directions

1. Place carrots in bottom of slow cooker. Place pork on carrots and brush with preserves.

2. Cover; cook on LOW 8 hours or on HIGH 4 hours.

Makes 4 servings

glazed pork loin

garlic-pepper steak

1¼ teaspoons LAWRY'S®
Garlic Powder With
Parsley

1 pound sirloin steak

1¼ teaspoons LAWRY'S®
Seasoned Pepper

½ teaspoon LAWRY'S®
Seasoned Salt

Press Garlic Powder With Parsley into both sides of steak with back of spoon. Sprinkle both sides with Seasoned Pepper and Seasoned Salt. Cover and refrigerate for 30 minutes; grill or broil for about 4 to 7 minutes per side or until desired doneness.

Makes 4 servings

Meal Idea: Serve with hot baked potatoes and a crisp green salad.

Prep. Time: 3 to 4 minutes
Cook Time: 8 to 14 minutes

asian-seasoned barbecue pork sandwiches

1 large (17×15 inches)
foil cooking bag

1½ pounds lean pork
stew meat, cut into
1½-inch pieces

¾ cup barbecue sauce

¼ cup teriyaki marinade

2 tablespoons honey

2 tablespoons all-
purpose flour

½ teaspoon hot pepper
sauce

6 hamburger buns

1. Prepare grill for direct cooking.

2. Place bag in 1-inch deep jelly-roll pan. Toss together meat, barbecue sauce, marinade, honey, flour and hot pepper sauce in large bowl. Spoon into bag, arranging in even layer. Double-fold open side of bag, leaving head space for heat circulation.

3. Slide bag from pan onto grill grid. Grill, covered, over medium coals 15 to 20 minutes or until meat is tender. Carefully open bag. Transfer mixture to bowl. Using two forks, coarsely shred pork. Stir pork together with sauce. Serve on buns.

Makes 6 servings

italian beef

1 beef rump roast (3 to 5 pounds)

1 can (14 ounces) beef broth

2 cups mild giardiniera

8 Italian bread rolls

Slow Cooker Directions

1. Place rump roast in slow cooker; add beef broth and giardiniera.

2. Cover; cook on LOW 10 hours.

3. Shred beef; serve with sauce on crusty Italian rolls.

Makes 8 servings

slow cooker beef stew

¼ cup all-purpose flour

½ teaspoon salt

½ teaspoon pepper

1 beef round steak, cut into ¾-inch pieces (about 2 pounds)

2 tablespoons vegetable oil

1½ cups water

1 package (about 1 ounce) beef stew seasoning mix

4 medium potatoes, cut in ½-inch dice

3 cups sliced carrots

½ cup chopped onion

1 can (14½ ounces) low-sodium beef broth

Slow Cooker Directions

1. Combine flour, salt and pepper. Coat beef with seasoned flour. Heat oil in large skillet. Brown beef in batches. Add seasoning mix and water; mix well.

2. Place potatoes, carrots and onion into slow cooker. Top with beef mixture; add beef broth. Cover; cook on LOW 6 to 8 hours or until vegetables are tender.

Makes 6 servings

italian beef

80

cowboy burgers

1 **pound ground beef or turkey**

½ **teaspoon LAWRY'S® Seasoned Salt**

½ **teaspoon LAWRY'S® Seasoned Pepper**

3 **tablespoons butter or margarine**

1 **large onion, thinly sliced**

1 **package (1 ounce) LAWRY'S® Taco Spices & Seasonings**

4 **slices cheddar cheese**

4 **Kaiser rolls**

Lettuce leaves

Tomato slices

In medium bowl, combine ground beef, Seasoned Salt and Seasoned Pepper; shape into four patties. Grill or broil to desired doneness. Meanwhile, in medium skillet, melt butter. Mix in onion and Taco Spices & Seasoning. Cook onion until soft and transparent. Top each patty with cheese and onions. Return to grill or broiler until cheese is melted. Place each patty on roll; top with lettuce and tomato. *Makes 4 servings*

Meal Idea: Serve with your favorite baked beans.

Prep. Time: 5 minutes
Cook Time: 7 to 10 minutes

cowboy burger

82

tuscan steak and beans

⅓ cup balsamic vinegar

3 cloves garlic, minced

2¼ pounds boneless top loin sirloin steak, cut into six 6-ounce steaks

1 tablespoon dried oregano leaves

6 sheets (15×12 inches) heavy-duty foil, lightly sprayed with nonstick cooking spray

1 package (16 ounces) frozen lima beans

1 package (8 ounces) sliced mushrooms

1½ teaspoons salt

1½ teaspoons black pepper

1 lemon, cut lengthwise into 6 wedges

1. Preheat oven to 450°F.

2. Combine vinegar and garlic in large resealable plastic food storage bag; add steaks. Seal bag; turn to coat steaks.

3. Remove steaks from marinade; discard remaining marinade. Sprinkle ½ teaspoon oregano in center of one foil sheet. Lay 1 steak on top. Spoon about ½ cup lima beans over half of steak. Sprinkle about ½ cup sliced mushrooms over other half of steak. Sprinkle steak and vegetables with ¼ teaspoon salt and ¼ teaspoon pepper. Double fold sides and ends of foil to seal packet, leaving head space for heat circulation. Repeat with remaining foil, oregano, steaks, lima beans, mushrooms, salt and pepper. Place packets on baking sheet.

4. Bake 25 to 30 minutes. Let stand 5 minutes. Carefully open packets and transfer contents to serving plates. Top each steak with lemon wedge.

Makes 6 servings

Note: Steaks can be prepared on grill. Prepare grill for direct cooking. Continue as directed above. Grill, covered, 16 minutes.

steaks with zesty merlot sauce

½ cup merlot wine

2 tablespoons Worcestershire sauce

1 tablespoon balsamic vinegar

1 teaspoon sugar

1 teaspoon beef bouillon granules

½ teaspoon dried thyme leaves

2 beef ribeye steaks (8 ounces each)

2 tablespoons finely chopped parsley

1. Combine wine, Worcestershire sauce, vinegar, sugar, bouillon granules and thyme; set aside.

2. Heat large nonstick skillet over high heat until hot. Add steaks; cook 3 minutes on each side. Turn steaks again and cook 3 to 6 minutes longer over medium heat or until desired doneness.

3. Cut steaks in half; arrange on serving platter. Place in oven to keep warm.

4. Add wine mixture to same skillet. Bring to a boil; cook and stir 1 minute, scraping up any brown bits. Spoon over steaks. Sprinkle with parsley; serve immediately. *Makes 4 servings*

steaks with zesty merlot sauce

spicy pork stir-fry

1 can (14½ ounces) fat-free reduced-sodium chicken broth, divided

2 tablespoons cornstarch

2 tablespoons reduced-sodium soy sauce

1 tablespoon grated orange peel

1 lean pork tenderloin (about 10 ounces), trimmed of visible fat

2 tablespoons peanut oil, divided

1 tablespoon sesame seeds

2 cloves garlic, minced

2 cups broccoli florets

2 cups sliced carrots

1 teaspoon Szechwan seasoning

3 cups hot cooked white rice

1. Combine 1½ cups chicken broth, cornstarch, soy sauce and orange peel in medium bowl. Cut pork lengthwise, then crosswise into ¼-inch-thick slices.

2. Heat 1 tablespoon oil in wok over high heat until hot. Add pork, sesame seeds and garlic. Stir-fry 3 minutes or until pork is barely pink in center. Remove from wok.

3. Heat remaining 1 tablespoon oil in wok until hot. Add broccoli, carrots, Szechwan seasoning and remaining chicken broth. Cook and stir 5 minutes or until vegetables are crisp-tender. Add pork. Stir chicken broth mixture and add to wok. Cook and stir over medium heat until sauce thickens. Serve over rice.

Makes 6 servings

Prep and Cook Time: 30 minutes

helpful hint

When grating orange peel, grate only the outer orange layer of the skin, which is very sweet and flavorful. Avoid grating into the white pith, as it has a bitter taste.

POULTRY BASICS

Weeknight meals or even a dinner party for ten will be easy to prepare when you choose poultry as your main dish. Chicken and turkey are the two types of poultry featured in this chapter—both are simple to cook. There are so many great ways to fix them, you will never run out of ideas. Best of all, some poultry cuts are inexpensive and lower in fat than beef and pork. Whether you're cooking Easy Chicken Alfredo (page 98) or Herbed Turkey Breast with Orange Sauce (page 116) you will enjoy your meal and the time spent cooking it.

POULTRY & SALMONELLA

Poultry, especially chicken, may be contaminated with salmonella bacteria, a harmful microorganism that causes food poisoning, so careful handling is essential. Do not let the juices from uncooked poultry mingle with other foods, either in the grocery cart at the store, in the refrigerator or on the counter at home. Wash any surfaces and utensils, including your hands, that have come in contact with raw poultry, using hot, soapy water. Always cook poultry thoroughly; do not partially cook it and then store it to finish cooking later. Care also needs to be taken when transporting, storing and thawing poultry.

CHICKEN

Types of Chicken

•Broiler-fryers are the smallest, most common and the most economical. As the name indicates, they are intended for frying and broiling but can also be used for braising, baking, grilling and poaching. They are young, usually 7 to 10 weeks old, and weigh from 1½ to 3½ pounds. They are sold whole or cut into parts.

•Roasters are larger chickens that weigh from 4 to 7 pounds. Slightly older than broiler-fryers (about 16 weeks old), they have more fat, making them well-suited for oven roasting and rotisserie cooking. They usually are sold whole.

Cuts of Chicken
•Cut-up chickens are whole chickens that have generally been cut into eight pieces: two breast halves, thighs, legs and wings. Whole chickens, whether whole or cut-up, contain the giblets (neck, gizzard, liver and heart). Be sure to remove them before cooking.

•Chicken breasts, the white meat of the chicken, are a popular cut and one of the more costly. Breasts are available whole, with both skin and bone intact. They can also be purchased with the bone removed but the skin intact or with the skin and bone both removed. The breast is often split. Recipe references to chicken breasts usually mean a chicken breast half. Split skinless and boneless breasts are convenient, but those that are cooked on the bone often result in a juicier and more flavorful dish. After removing and discarding the skin, the chicken does not have any more fat than chicken cooked without the skin.

•Other cuts include legs, also called drumsticks, wings and ground chicken. Legs can be sold separately, but many are still attached to the thigh. Thighs also are available separately. Wings, also called drumettes, are available. These are used for appetizers or main dishes, often marinated and baked.

TURKEY

Types of Turkey
Almost all turkeys sold in the United States are of the White Holland variety, a type that is bred to have mild, juicy meat with a high proportion of white meat. Toms (male) and hens (female) are available. Hens are somewhat smaller on the average. Fresh and frozen turkeys are available. Both can be of excellent quality. Many are self-basting, which helps to keep the breast meat moist. If fat content is a consideration, read the ingredient list carefully because some turkeys are basted with butter or vegetable oil. Those with broth are lower in fat.

Cuts of Turkey
•Turkey breasts, sold whole or as halves, are available with the bone in, boned and rolled, as boneless halves, and as breast cutlets. Except for the cutlets, the breast parts can be roasted, stewed, braised or cut into pieces and used in stews. Cutlets can be sautéed or braised.

•Drumsticks and thighs also are available. They can be prepared by the same methods as the breast parts.

•Fresh ground turkey is sold in most supermarkets and can be used in place of ground beef in many recipes. It has soared in popularity due to a lower fat content. Read the label carefully; if skin or fat is ground along with the meat, the amount of fat and cholesterol will increase. Processed turkey includes turkey sausage, turkey franks, and traditional deli and luncheon meats.

BUYING FRESH POULTRY

Choose poultry that is plump looking and has no unpleasant odors. Packaging should be free of tears. Check the "freshness date" on the package, which indicates the last sale date. Poultry should keep at least two days beyond this date.

STORING FRESH POULTRY

•Fresh, uncooked poultry can be refrigerated for up to two days. If the poultry you purchase comes packaged in plastic bags or on plastic-sealed trays, it may be refrigerated in the original packaging. When you are ready to cook the poultry, rinse it under cold water, pat it dry with paper towels and trim away any excess fat.

•Poultry should be stored in the coldest part of the refrigerator and used within two days after its "last sale date."

• If the poultry you purchase will not be cooked within two days, it should be frozen. To properly freeze poultry, remove it from its original packaging. Rinse it under cold water, pat it dry with paper towels and trim away excess fat. For a whole chicken or turkey, remove the giblets from the body cavity. Freeze whole birds for up to eight months, pieces for up to six months and giblets for up to three months.

THAWING FROZEN POULTRY

•The best way to defrost uncooked frozen poultry, whether in pieces or a whole bird, is to thaw it in its wrapping in the refrigerator.

•Allow enough time for it to thaw completely, about three to four hours per pound for a whole chicken, chicken pieces or turkey pieces. When thawing a whole turkey, remember that this is a lengthy process, taking as long as four days for a large 25-pound bird. Estimate 24 hours of thawing time for every 5 pounds of bird.

•Never defrost poultry on the countertop at room temperature. The outside will thaw before the inside, increasing the possibility of bacterial growth on the thawed portions.

PREPARING POULTRY

•For bone-in chicken pieces, rinse them under cold running water to remove surface dirt and bone fragments.

•For boneless chicken breasts, each breast half has a white tendon that runs down the length of the underside. This toughens as it cooks so you may wish to remove it when possible. To do so, grasp it at one end and use a paring knife to scrape it away from the flesh.

•For a whole chicken, rinse it under cold running water and drain well. Most cooks remove all excess visible fat. Clumps of fat tend to gather around the neck and tail and can be removed by tugging them with your fingers or trimming them with kitchen shears or a utility knife.

•Some recipes call for flattening chicken breasts, usually to ¼ inch, so they can be filled and rolled or cooked more quickly. To flatten uncooked boneless chicken breasts, place one chicken breast half between two sheets of waxed paper or plastic wrap. Using the flat side of a meat mallet or a rolling pin, gently pound the chicken from the center to the outside until it is of the desired thickness.

•For a whole frozen turkey, after thawing, remove the giblets from the neck and body cavities. Wash the inside and outside of the turkey under cold water and drain well. Do not stuff the turkey until you are ready to cook it.

COOKING POULTRY

There are many cooking methods that can be applied to chicken and turkey. One of the most successful is roasting a whole chicken. Bone-in chicken parts can be broiled, poached, grilled, braised or baked. Boneless cuts can be prepared in the same way. In addition, they can be sautéed, panfried or stir-fried. In other words, almost any cooking method works. Because chicken has a mild flavor, marinades or dry rubs are welcome additions. The purpose of this step is not to tenderize, since the meat already is tender, but to add flavor. Therefore, keep in mind that marinating can be completed in 20 to 30 minutes. Chicken should not be left in acidic marinades for more than 2 hours or the acid will break down the tissue and the flesh will become mushy.

TESTING FOR DONENESS

•There are a number of ways to determine if chicken is thoroughly cooked and ready to eat. For a whole chicken, a meat thermometer inserted into the thickest part of the thigh, but not near any bone or fat, should register 180°F before removing the chicken from the oven. If a whole chicken is stuffed, insert an instant-read thermometer into the center of the body cavity; when the stuffing registers 165°F, it is done. Roasted whole chicken breasts are done when they register 170°F on a meat thermometer. For bone-in chicken pieces, it should be easy to insert a fork into the chicken and the juices should run clear; however, the meat and juices nearest the bones might still be a little pink even though the chicken is cooked. Boneless chicken pieces are done when the centers are no longer pink; determine this by simply cutting into the chicken with a knife.

•For a whole turkey, follow the doneness test of a whole chicken. However, it is also essential to check the temperature of the thigh. The pop-up timers that are on some turkeys should only be used only as a guide. Rely on a meat thermometer for an accurate indication of the internal temperature.

ENTICING POULTRY

....

chicken teriyaki

8 large chicken
  drumsticks (about
  2 pounds)

⅓ cup teriyaki sauce

2 tablespoons brandy or
  apple juice

1 green onion, minced

1 tablespoon vegetable
  oil

1 teaspoon ground
  ginger

½ teaspoon sugar

¼ teaspoon garlic
  powder

  Prepared sweet and
  sour sauce
  (optional)

1. Remove skin from drumsticks, if desired, by pulling skin toward end of leg using paper towel; discard skin.

2. Place chicken in large resealable plastic food storage bag. Combine teriyaki sauce, brandy, onion, oil, ginger, sugar and garlic powder in small bowl; pour over chicken. Close bag securely, turning to coat. Marinate in refrigerator at least 1 hour or overnight, turning occasionally.

3. Prepare grill for indirect cooking.

4. Drain chicken; reserve marinade. Place chicken on grid directly over drip pan. Grill, covered, over medium-high heat 60 minutes or until chicken is no longer pink in center and juices run clear, turning and brushing with reserved marinade every 20 minutes. *Do not brush with marinade during last 5 minutest of grilling.* Discard remaining marinade. Serve with sweet and sour sauce, if desired.   *Makes 4 servings*

chicken teriyaki

91

peppy pesto toss

8 ounces uncooked ziti or mostaccioli

1 package (16 ounces) frozen bell pepper and onion strips, thawed

½ pound deli turkey breast or smoked turkey breast, cut ½ inch thick

1 cup half-and-half

½ cup pesto sauce

¼ cup grated Parmesan or Asiago cheese

1. Cook pasta according to package directions.

2. Add pepper and onion mixture to pasta water during last 2 minutes of cooking. Meanwhile, cut turkey into ½-inch cubes.

3. Drain pasta and vegetables in colander.

4. Combine half-and-half, pesto sauce and turkey in saucepan used to prepare pasta. Cook 2 minutes or until heated through.

5. Return pasta and vegetables to saucepan and toss well to coat. Sprinkle with grated cheese. Serve immediately. *Makes 4 servings*

Prep and Cook Time: 20 minutes

buffalo chicken sandwiches

2 tablespoons butter or margarine

Juice of one lemon (3 to 4 tablespoons)

4 to 8 dashes hot pepper sauce to taste

1 package (about 1 pound) PERDUE® FIT 'N EASY® Skinless & Boneless Chicken Breasts

1 loaf (10 ounces) frozen garlic bread

4 tablespoons prepared blue cheese dressing

Prepare outdoor grill for cooking or preheat broiler. In small saucepan over low heat, melt butter with lemon juice and hot sauce. Coat chicken with seasoned butter; grill or broil 5 to 6 inches from heat source 6 to 8 minutes per side, until cooked through. Meanwhile, warm bread following package directions. Cut bread into 4 sandwich-sized slices. Place chicken on bottom layer of bread. Top chicken with 1 tablespoon blue cheese dressing and remaining bread.

Makes 4 servings

Prep Time: 5 minutes
Cook Time: 15 to 20 minutes

peppy pesto toss

california turkey burgers

1 pound ground turkey

½ cup finely chopped cilantro

⅓ cup plain dry bread crumbs

3 tablespoons *French's*® Classic Yellow® Mustard

1 egg, beaten

½ teaspoon salt

¼ teaspoon black pepper

8 thin slices (3 ounces) Monterey Jack cheese

½ red or yellow bell pepper, seeded and cut into rings

4 hamburger buns

1. Combine turkey, cilantro, bread crumbs, mustard, egg, salt and pepper in large bowl. Shape into 4 patties, pressing firmly.

2. Place patties on oiled grid. Grill over high heat 15 minutes or until no longer pink in center. Top burgers with cheese during last few minutes of grilling. Grill pepper rings 2 minutes. To serve, place burgers on buns and top with pepper rings. Serve with additional mustard, if desired.   *Makes 4 servings*

Prep Time: 15 minutes
Cook Time: 15 minutes

helpful hint

Cilantro is a fresh leafy herb that looks a lot like Italian parsley. Its distinctive flavor complements spicy foods, especially Mexican, Caribbean, Thai and Vietnamese dishes.

california turkey burger

grilled tuscan chicken sandwich

4 boneless skinless
   chicken breast
   halves

2 tablespoons olive oil

2 tablespoons MRS.
   DASH® Tomato
   Basil Garlic
   seasoning

½ cup sliced green olives

½ cup light mayonnaise

4 large crusty rolls

4 large romaine lettuce
   leaves, washed and
   patted dry, torn in
   half crosswise

4 slices roasted red
   peppers, from a jar
   or deli counter

Preheat grill to medium-high. Brush chicken breasts with olive oil on each side and sprinkle with Mrs. Dash Tomato Basil Garlic seasoning. Grill for 5 minutes, turn, and grill for another 5 minutes, or until juices run clear when a skewer is inserted. Remove and cool slightly. In a bowl, mix sliced olives and mayonnaise. Cut rolls in half and spread the olive mixture on each side of each roll. Layer lettuce leaf half, chicken breast, roasted red pepper slice and other half of lettuce leaf on each of bottom roll half, and place other half of roll on top. Serve immediately. *Makes 4 servings*

Preparation Time: 10 minutes
Cooking Time: 12 minutes

helpful hint

Prepare these sandwiches for an afternoon barbecue or a picnic in the park. Serve with a prepared pasta salad.

chicken pomodoro with tomato basil garlic

4 teaspoons olive oil

8 boneless skinless chicken breast halves

8 ounces fresh mushrooms, sliced

2 cans (14¼ ounces) Italian-style stewed tomatoes

8 teaspoons MRS. DASH® Tomato Basil Garlic seasoning

½ cup semi-dry white wine (optional)

Heat oil in nonstick skillet. Add chicken and brown over medium heat, about 10 minutes, turning once. Add remaining ingredients. Bring to a boil; reduce heat and simmer, uncovered, 15 minutes. *Makes 8 servings*

Preparation Time: 10 minutes
Cooking Time: 25 minutes

helpful hint

Serve the chicken over hot cooked white rice or pasta.

basic turkey burger

1 pound ground turkey

½ cup seasoned dry bread crumbs

⅓ cup finely chopped onion

1 egg, beaten

1 teaspoon soy sauce

1 teaspoon Worcestershire sauce

½ teaspoon garlic powder

¼ teaspoon dry mustard

1. In large bowl combine turkey, bread crumbs, onion, egg, soy sauce, Worcestershire sauce, garlic powder and mustard.

2. Shape meat mixture into 4 patties, each ½ inch thick. On lightly greased broiling pan, about 4 inches from heat, broil burgers 5 minutes per side, until internal temperature reaches 165°F or until no longer pink in center. *Makes 4 servings*

*Favorite recipe from **National Turkey Federation***

easy chicken alfredo

1½ pounds chicken breast, cut into ½-inch pieces

1 medium onion, chopped

1 tablespoon dried chives

1 tablespoon dried basil leaves

1 tablespoon extra-virgin olive oil

1 teaspoon lemon pepper

¼ teaspoon ground ginger

½ pound broccoli, coarsely chopped

1 red bell pepper, chopped

1 can (8 ounces) sliced water chestnuts, drained

1 cup baby carrots

3 cloves garlic, minced

1 jar (16 ounces) Alfredo sauce

1 package (8 ounces) wide egg noodles, cooked and drained

Slow Cooker Directions

1. Combine chicken, onion, chives, basil, olive oil, lemon pepper and ginger in slow cooker; stir thoroughly. Add broccoli, bell pepper, water chestnuts, carrots and garlic. Mix well.

2. Cover; cook on LOW 8 hours or on HIGH 3 hours.

3. Add Alfredo sauce and cook on HIGH an additional 30 minutes or until heated through.

4. Serve over hot egg noodles.   *Makes 6 servings*

helpful hint

Dairy products should be added at the end of the cooking time because they will curdle if cooked in the slow cooker for a long time.

easy chicken alfredo

south of the border turkey kabobs

1 package
   BUTTERBALL®
   Fresh Boneless
   Turkey Breast
   Medallions

¼ cup vegetable oil

¼ cup fresh lime juice

2 teaspoons salt

1 teaspoon chili powder

½ teaspoon garlic
   powder

2 medium yellow
   squash, cut into
   ¾-inch chunks

2 medium onions, cut
   into ¾-inch chunks

2 red bell peppers, cut
   into ¾-inch chunks

2 green bell peppers, cut
   into ¾-inch chunks

Combine oil, lime juice, salt, chili powder and garlic powder in large bowl. Toss vegetables in oil mixture; stir to coat. Transfer vegetables to separate large bowl. Add turkey medallions to oil mixture; stir to coat. Thread turkey and vegetables alternately onto skewers, leaving a small space between pieces. Grill over hot coals about 20 minutes or until turkey is no longer pink in center, turning occasionally to prevent burning.

Makes 6 servings

Prep Time: 30 minutes

helpful hint

If using wooden skewers, soak them in water for 30 minutes to prevent burning while cooking.

south of the border turkey kabobs

chicken and vegetable pasta

8 ounces (4 cups) uncooked bowtie pasta

2 red or green bell peppers, seeded and cut into quarters

1 medium zucchini, cut into halves

3 boneless skinless chicken breasts (about 1 pound)

½ cup Italian dressing

½ cup prepared pesto sauce

1. Cook pasta according to package directions. Drain; place in large bowl. Cover to keep warm.

2. While pasta is cooking, combine vegetables, chicken and dressing in medium bowl; toss well. Grill or broil 6 to 8 minutes on each side or until vegetables are crisp-tender and chicken is no longer pink in center. (Vegetables may take less time than chicken.)

3. Cut vegetables and chicken into bite-size pieces. Add vegetables, chicken and pesto to pasta; toss well.

Makes 4 to 6 servings

Prep and Cook Time: 20 minutes

chicken and vegetable pasta

dad's favorite turkey kabobs

3 ears corn, cut into
  1-inch pieces

2 medium zucchini, cut
  into ¾-inch pieces

2 red bell peppers, cut
  into 1-inch squares

2 turkey tenderloins
  (about 1 pound), cut
  into 1-inch cubes

⅓ cup reduced-calorie
  Italian salad
  dressing

  Additional reduced-
  calorie Italian salad
  dressing

In medium saucepan over high heat, blanch corn in boiling water about 1 to 2 minutes. Remove corn from saucepan and plunge into cold water.

In large glass bowl, toss corn, zucchini, peppers, turkey and ⅓ cup dressing; cover and refrigerate 1 to 2 hours.

Drain turkey and vegetables, discarding marinade. Alternately thread turkey cubes and vegetables on 8 skewers, leaving ½-inch space between turkey and vegetables.

On outdoor charcoal grill, cook kabobs 18 to 20 minutes, brushing with additional dressing. Turn skewers after first 10 minutes.

Makes 4 servings (8 kabobs)

*Favorite recipe from **National Turkey Federation***

spicy chicken fingers

1 cup instant mashed
  potato flakes

2 HERB-OX® spicy
  chicken flavored
  bouillon cubes,
  crushed

¼ cup butter or
  margarine, melted

1 egg, beaten

2 tablespoons water

1¼ pounds boneless,
  skinless, chicken
  breast tenders

Preheat oven to 400°F. In bowl, combine potato flakes and bouillon. Add melted butter to potato flakes. In pie plate, combine egg and water. Dip chicken tenders in egg mixture and coat in potato flakes. Place chicken on baking sheet. Bake for 18 to 22 minutes, turning halfway through baking, until chicken is cooked through. If desired, serve with honey mustard dipping sauce and coleslaw. *Makes 4 servings*

Prep Time: 10 minutes
Total Time: 35 minutes

grilled chicken, rice & veggies

2 boneless skinless
chicken breasts
(about 3 ounces
each)

¼ cup plus 2 tablespoons
reduced-fat Italian
salad dressing,
divided

1 cup fat-free reduced-
sodium chicken
broth

½ cup uncooked rice

1 cup frozen broccoli
and carrot blend,
thawed

helpful hint

*The longer chicken stays
in the marinade, the more
flavor it will have. Turn
the chicken occasionally
so the marinade
penetrates evenly.*

1. Place chicken and 2 tablespoons salad dressing in resealable plastic food storage bag. Seal bag; turn to coat. Marinate in refrigerator 1 hour.

2. Remove chicken from marinade; discard marinade. Grill chicken over medium-hot coals 8 to 10 minutes or until chicken is no longer pink in center.

3. Meanwhile, bring broth to a boil in small saucepan; add rice. Cover; reduce heat and simmer 15 minutes, stirring in vegetables during last 5 minutes of cooking. Remove from heat and stir in remaining ¼ cup dressing. Serve with chicken. *Makes 2 servings*

grilled chicken, rice & veggies

saucy tomato chicken

6 ounces uncooked yolk-free egg noodles

1 can (14½ ounces) stewed tomatoes with onions, celery and green bell pepper

2 cloves garlic, minced

1 teaspoon dried oregano leaves

Nonstick cooking spray

4 boneless skinless chicken breasts, rinsed and patted dry, (4 ounces each)

2 teaspoons olive oil

1. Cook noodles according to package directions, omitting salt and oil; drain.

2. Meanwhile, heat large nonstick skillet over high heat; add tomatoes, garlic and oregano. Bring to a boil over high heat; boil 5 minutes, stirring constantly, or until liquid is reduced and tomato mixture becomes slightly darker in color. This allows the sugars to caramelize and gives the tomatoes a deep concentrated flavor. (Mixture will be thick.) Transfer to small bowl and keep warm. Wipe out skillet.

3. Spray same skillet with cooking spray. Add chicken and cook 6 minutes. Turn; reduce heat to medium-low. Spoon tomato mixture into skillet around chicken. Cover and cook 4 minutes or until chicken is no longer pink in center and juices run clear.

4. Remove skillet from heat. Place noodles on serving platter and top with chicken pieces. Add olive oil to tomato mixture in skillet and stir well to blend. Spoon equal amounts of tomato mixture over each piece of chicken. *Makes 4 servings*

saucy tomato chicken

saucy tropical turkey

3 to 4 turkey thighs, skin removed (about 2½ pounds)

2 tablespoons cooking oil

1 small onion, halved and sliced

1 can (20 ounces) pineapple chunks, drained

1 red bell pepper, cubed

⅔ cup apricot preserves

3 tablespoons soy sauce

1 teaspoon grated lemon peel

1 teaspoon ground ginger

¼ cup cold water

2 tablespoons cornstarch

Hot cooked rice or noodles

Slow Cooker Directions

1. Rinse turkey and pat dry. Heat oil in large skillet; brown turkey on all sides. Place onion in slow cooker. Transfer turkey to slow cooker and top with pineapple and bell pepper.

2. Combine preserves, soy sauce, lemon peel and ginger in small bowl; mix well. Spoon over turkey. Cover; cook on LOW 6 to 7 hours.

3. Remove turkey from slow cooker; keep warm. Blend water and cornstarch until smooth; stir into slow cooker. Cook on HIGH 15 minutes or until sauce is slightly thickened. Adjust seasonings, if desired. Return turkey to slow cooker; cook until hot. Serve with rice.

Makes 6 servings

Prep Time: 15 minutes
Cook Time: 6½ to 7½ hours

> ## helpful hint
>
> *Browning meats and poultry and draining the fat is another way to help reduce fat in slow cooker dishes.*

saucy tropical turkey

pesto-coated baked chicken

1 pound boneless skinless chicken breasts, cut into ½-inch thick cutlets

¼ cup plus 1 tablespoon prepared pesto

1½ teaspoons reduced-fat sour cream

1½ teaspoons reduced-fat mayonnaise

1 tablespoon shredded Parmesan cheese

1 tablespoon pine nuts

1. Preheat oven to 450°F. Arrange chicken in single layer in shallow baking pan. Combine pesto, sour cream and mayonnaise in small cup. Brush over chicken. Sprinkle with cheese and pine nuts.

2. Bake 8 to 10 minutes or until cooked through.

Makes 4 servings

Variation: Chicken can be cooked on an oiled grid over a preheated grill.

pesto-coated baked chicken

indonesian grilled turkey with satay sauce

2 disposable aluminum foil pans (9 inches each)

1 whole turkey breast (about 5 pounds)

2 tablespoons *French's*® Worcestershire Sauce

2 tablespoons olive oil

2 teaspoons seasoned salt

½ teaspoon ground black pepper

Satay Sauce (recipe follows)

helpful hint

Cleanup is easier if the grill rack is coated with vegetable oil or nonstick cooking spray before grilling.

To prepare grill, place doubled foil pans in center of grill under grilling rack. Arrange hot coals or lava rocks around foil pan. Fill pan with cold water. Place turkey on greased grid. Combine Worcestershire, oil and seasonings in small bowl; brush generously on turkey.

Grill, on covered grill, over medium-low to medium coals 1½ hours or until meat thermometer inserted into turkey reaches 170°F. Slice turkey. Serve with Satay Sauce.   *Makes 8 servings*

satay sauce

½ cup chunky-style peanut butter

⅓ cup *French's*® Worcestershire Sauce

¼ cup loosely packed fresh cilantro leaves

2 tablespoons *Frank's*® *RedHot*® Original Cayenne Pepper Sauce

2 tablespoons sugar

2 tablespoons water

1 tablespoon chopped peeled fresh ginger

2 cloves garlic, chopped

Place peanut butter, Worcestershire, cilantro, **Frank's RedHot** Sauce, sugar, water, ginger and garlic in food processor or blender. Cover and process until smooth.
Makes 1⅓ cups

Prep Time: 20 minutes
Cook Time: 1 hour 30 minutes

chicken, stuffing & green bean bake

1 package (7 ounces) cubed herb-seasoned stuffing

4 sheets (18×12 inches) heavy-duty foil, lightly sprayed with nonstick cooking spray

½ cup chicken broth

3 cups frozen cut green beans

4 boneless skinless chicken breasts

1 cup chicken gravy

⅛ teaspoon black pepper

Additional chicken gravy, heated (optional)

1. Preheat oven to 450°F.

2. Place ¼ of stuffing (1 scant cup) on one sheet of foil. Pour 2 tablespoons chicken broth over stuffing. Top stuffing with ¾ cup green beans. Place one chicken breast on top of beans. Combine gravy and pepper; pour ¼ cup over chicken.

3. Double fold sides and ends of foil to seal packet, leaving head space for heat circulation. Repeat with remaining foil, stuffing, broth, beans, chicken and gravy mixture to make three more packets. Place packets on baking sheet.

4. Bake 20 minutes or until chicken is no longer pink in center. Remove from oven. Carefully open one end of each packet to allow steam to escape. Open packets and transfer contents to serving plates. Serve with additional gravy, if desired. *Makes 4 servings*

chicken, stuffing & green bean bake

classic chicken parmesan

6 boneless, skinless chicken breast halves, pounded thin (about 1½ pounds)

2 eggs, lightly beaten

1 cup Italian seasoned dry bread crumbs

2 tablespoons olive oil

1 jar (1 pound 10 ounces) RAGÚ® Old World Style® Pasta Sauce

1 cup shredded mozzarella cheese (about 4 ounces)

Preheat oven to 375°F. Dip chicken in eggs, then bread crumbs, coating well.

In 12-inch skillet, heat olive oil over medium-high heat and brown chicken; drain on paper towels.

In 11×7-inch baking dish, evenly spread 1 cup Ragú Old World Style Pasta Sauce. Arrange chicken in dish. Top with remaining sauce. Sprinkle with mozzarella cheese and, if desired, grated Parmesan cheese. Bake uncovered 25 minutes or until chicken is thoroughly cooked. *Makes 6 servings*

helpful hint

To pound chicken, place a boneless, skinless breast between two sheets of waxed paper. Use a rolling pin to press down and out from the center to flatten.

classic chicken parmesan

herbed turkey breast with orange sauce

1 large onion, chopped

3 cloves garlic, minced

1 teaspoon dried rosemary

½ teaspoon black pepper

2 to 3 pounds boneless skinless turkey breast

1½ cups orange juice

Slow Cooker Directions

1. Place onion in slow cooker. Combine garlic, rosemary and pepper in small bowl; set aside. Cut slices about three-fourths of the way through turkey at 2-inch intervals. Rub garlic mixture between slices.

2. Place turkey, cut side up, in slow cooker. Pour orange juice over turkey. Cover; cook on LOW 7 to 8 hours or until internal temperature reaches 170°F when tested with meat thermometer inserted into the thickest part of breast.

3. Transfer turkey to cutting board; cover with foil and let stand 10 to 15 minutes before carving. Internal temperature will rise 5° to 10°F during stand time. Serve sauce mixture from slow cooker with sliced turkey.

Makes 4 to 6 servings

crispy oven fried chicken

1 cup dry breadcrumbs

2½ teaspoons LAWRY'S® Seasoned Salt

¾ teaspoon LAWRY'S® Seasoned Pepper

1 cup buttermilk

3½ pounds chicken pieces

In large resealable plastic bag, combine breadcrumbs, Seasoned Salt and Seasoned Pepper; shake. Pour buttermilk into shallow dish. Dip chicken pieces into buttermilk then place in bag; shake to coat. Spray 13×9×2-inch baking dish with nonstick cooking spray; arrange chicken pieces, skin-side-up. Bake, uncovered, in 400°F oven until chicken is thoroughly cooked, about 1 hour.

Makes 6 servings

Prep. Time: 12 to 15 minutes
Cook Time: 1 hour

herbed turkey breast
with orange sauce

country herb roasted chicken

1 chicken (2½ to 3 pounds), cut into serving pieces (with or without skin) *or* 1½ pounds boneless skinless chicken breast halves

1 envelope LIPTON® RECIPE SECRETS® Savory Herb with Garlic Soup Mix

2 tablespoons water

1 tablespoon BERTOLLI® Olive Oil

1. Preheat oven to 375°F.

2. In 13×9-inch baking or roasting pan, arrange chicken. In small bowl, combine remaining ingredients; brush on chicken.

3. For chicken pieces, bake uncovered 45 minutes or until chicken is thoroughly cooked. For chicken breast halves, bake uncovered 20 minutes or until chicken is thoroughly cooked. *Makes about 4 servings*

lemon-herb chicken

1 egg

½ cup dry bread crumbs

1½ teaspoons McCORMICK® Lemon & Pepper Seasoning

½ teaspoon McCORMICK® Dill Weed

1 pound boneless, skinless chicken breasts (4 half breasts)

2 tablespoons vegetable oil

1. Place egg in pie plate and beat lightly. Place bread crumbs on large piece of wax paper. Add seasoning and dill. Stir with fork until well combined.

2. Dip chicken breasts, 1 at a time, in beaten egg. Allow excess egg to drip off. Coat chicken evenly in bread crumb mixture.

3. Heat oil in skillet. Add coated chicken and sauté 5 to 6 minutes. Turn chicken over and cook 5 to 6 minutes or until no longer pink in center. Drain on paper towels. *Makes 4 servings*

country herb roasted chicken

crispy baked chicken

8 ounces (1 cup) fat-free French onion dip

½ cup fat-free (skim) milk

1 cup cornflake crumbs

½ cup wheat germ

6 skinless chicken breasts or thighs (about 1½ pounds)

1. Preheat oven to 350°F. Spray shallow baking pan with nonstick cooking spray.

2. Place dip in shallow bowl; stir until smooth. Add milk, 1 tablespoon at a time, until pourable consistency is reached.

3. Combine cornflake crumbs and wheat germ on plate.

4. Dip chicken pieces in dip mixture, then roll in cornflake mixture. Place chicken in single layer in prepared pan. Bake 45 to 50 minutes or until juices run clear when chicken is pierced with fork and chicken is no longer pink near bone. *Makes 6 servings*

quick chicken jambalaya

8 boneless, skinless chicken thighs, cut in bite-size pieces

¼ teaspoon garlic salt

1 tablespoon vegetable oil

2½ cups 8-vegetable juice

1 bag (16 ounces) frozen pepper stir-fry mix

½ cup diced cooked ham

1 teaspoon hot pepper sauce

1¾ cups quick cooking rice, uncooked

Sprinkle garlic salt over chicken. In large nonstick skillet, place oil and heat to medium-high temperature. Add chicken and cook, stirring occasionally, 8 minutes or until chicken is lightly browned. Add vegetable juice, pepper stir-fry mix, ham, and hot pepper sauce. Heat to boiling; cover and cook over medium heat 4 minutes. Stir in rice; heat to boiling. Cover, remove pan from heat and let stand 5 minutes or until rice and vegetables are tender and liquid is absorbed. *Makes 4 servings*

*Favorite recipe from **Delmarva Poultry Industry, Inc.***

crispy baked chicken

italian-style chicken and rice

1 tablespoon vegetable
   oil

4 boneless skinless
   chicken breasts
   (about 1 pound)

2 cups low-fat reduced-
   sodium chicken
   broth

1 box (about 6 ounces)
   chicken-flavored
   rice mix

½ cup chopped red bell
   pepper

½ cup frozen peas,
   thawed

¼ cup Romano cheese

1. Heat oil in large skillet. Add chicken; cook over medium-high heat 10 to 15 minutes or until lightly browned on both sides.

2. Add broth, rice mix, bell pepper and peas; mix well. Bring to a boil. Cover; reduce heat and simmer 10 minutes or until chicken is no longer pink in center. Remove from heat. Sprinkle with cheese; let stand covered 5 minutes or until liquid is absorbed.

Makes 4 servings

italian-style chicken and rice

quick & easy lasagna

1 package JENNIE-O
 TURKEY STORE®
 Hot or Sweet Lean
 Italian Sausage

1 jar (26 ounces) tomato
 and basil or
 mushroom spaghetti
 sauce

6 (7×4-inch) no-boil
 lasagna noodles

1 container (15 ounces)
 ricotta cheese

¼ cup grated Parmesan
 cheese

2 cups (8 ounces)
 shredded mozzarella
 cheese

Heat oven to 450°F. Crumble sausage into large saucepan; discard casings. Cook over medium-high heat 5 minutes, breaking sausage into chunks and stirring frequently. Add spaghetti sauce; bring to a boil. Reduce heat; simmer uncovered 5 minutes, stirring occasionally. Spread ¾ cup sauce in bottom of 9-inch square baking dish. Arrange 2 noodles side by side over sauce. Combine ricotta cheese and Parmesan cheese; spoon half of mixture over noodles and top with 1 cup sauce and ½ cup mozzarella cheese. Repeat layering with 2 more noodles, pressing firmly, remaining ricotta cheese mixture, 1 cup sauce, ½ cup mozzarella cheese and last 2 noodles, pressing firmly. Top with remaining sauce. Cover with foil; bake for 25 minutes or until noodles are tender and sauce is bubbly. Uncover; top with remaining 1 cup mozzarella cheese. Return to oven; bake 5 minutes or until cheese is melted. Let stand 5 minutes before serving. *Makes 6 servings*

Prep Time: 30 minutes
Cook Time: 30 minutes

roast chicken balsamic

1 PERDUE® OVEN
 STUFFER® Roaster

4 red onions, cut into
 wedges

1 cup balsamic
 vinaigrette

½ cup chicken broth

2 tablespoons fresh
 Italian parsley,
 chopped

Preheat oven to 350°F. Set chicken in a roasting dish and arrange onions around it. Pour vinaigrette and broth over chicken and onions. Roast until BIRD-WATCHER® Thermometer pops up and when meat thermometer inserted into the thickest part of thigh registers 180°F (approximately 2 hours).

Let chicken rest 10 minutes before carving and serving with onions. Garnish with parsley.

Makes 6 servings

spinach-stuffed turkey meatloaf

1 sheet (24×12 inches) heavy-duty foil

1 pound ground turkey

1 cup finely chopped onion

½ cup unseasoned dry breadcrumbs

½ cup finely chopped red bell pepper

2 eggs

2 tablespoons bacon bits

1 teaspoon dried thyme leaves

½ teaspoon salt

½ teaspoon black pepper

1 package (10 ounces) frozen chopped spinach, thawed and squeezed dry

⅓ cup sour cream

⅓ cup shredded Swiss cheese

1. Preheat oven to 450°F. Center foil over 9×5×3-inch loaf pan. Gently ease foil into pan; leaving a 1-inch overhang on sides of pan and 5-inch overhang on each end. Generously spray foil with nonstick cooking spray.

2. Combine turkey, onion, breadcrumbs, bell pepper, eggs, bacon bits, thyme, salt and black pepper in medium bowl; mix well.

3. Place about 3 cups turkey mixture into prepared pan, packing down lightly and making an indentation, end to end, with back of large spoon.

4. Combine spinach, sour cream and cheese in medium bowl. Spoon into indentation. Cover with remaining turkey mixture, packing down lightly. Fold foil over sides to cover completely; crimp foil, leaving head space for heat circulation.

5. Bake about 50 minutes or until cooked through. Let stand, covered, 10 minutes. Unwrap and slice into 1-inch slices. *Makes 8 servings*

spinach-stuffed turkey meatloaf

turkey fajitas

½ **cup sliced green
   onions**

½ **cup lemon juice**

½ **cup honey**

½ **cup warm water**

3 **tablespoons vegetable
   oil**

1 **clove garlic, minced**

1 **(1-pound) package
   turkey breast slices,
   cut into 2×¾-inch
   strips**

1 **medium yellow or
   green bell pepper,
   cut into strips**

1 **medium tomato,
   chopped**

½ **cup chopped fresh
   cilantro**

4 **(8-inch) flour tortillas**

   Picante sauce

Combine green onions, lemon juice, honey and water in small bowl; set aside. Heat oil and garlic in large skillet over medium-high heat. Add turkey; cook and stir for 2 minutes. Add pepper strips and lemon juice mixture; continue to cook and stir until liquid evaporates and turkey is golden brown. Stir in tomato and cilantro. Spoon mixture onto tortillas. Fold in half or roll up. Serve with picante sauce. *Makes 4 servings*

helpful hint

Serve the fajitas with guacamole, salsa and sour cream, if desired.

turkey fajitas

spanish rice & chicken skillet

1 tablespoon oil

4 chicken drumsticks
(about 1 pound)

1 onion, chopped

½ medium green bell
pepper, chopped

½ medium red bell
pepper, chopped

1 package (about
4 ounces) Spanish
rice mix

1 can (14½ ounces)
diced tomatoes,
undrained

1¼ cups chicken broth

1. Heat oil in medium skillet over high heat until hot. Add chicken; cook 5 minutes or until lightly browned on all sides. Add onion and bell peppers; cook and stir 2 minutes.

2. Stir in rice mix, tomatoes with juice and broth. Bring to a boil. Cover and simmer over low heat 15 minutes or until rice is tender and liquid is absorbed. Remove from heat and let stand, covered, 5 minutes.

Makes 4 servings

spanish rice & chicken skillet

hot open-faced turkey sandwiches

1 package JENNIE-O
  TURKEY STORE®
  Turkey Breast Slices,
  pounded to ¼-inch
  thickness

1 tablespoon olive or
  vegetable oil

4 or 5 large oval slices
  rye bread

¼ cup plain low-fat
  yogurt

1 tablespoon each
  prepared
  horseradish and
  brown mustard

1 large tomato, sliced

1 ripe avocado, pitted
  and sliced

1 red onion, sliced

1 to 1¼ cups shredded
  low-fat Co-jack
  cheese

Fresh greens or basil
  leaves (optional)

In medium skillet over medium heat, heat oil until hot. Cook pounded turkey slices for 1 to 2 minutes per side or until no longer pink. Set aside. Heat broiler; arrange bread on baking sheet and broil until lightly toasted. Mix yogurt, horseradish and mustard; spread half of mixture on bread slices. Lay slice of cooked turkey on each piece of bread. Layer tomato and avocado on turkey. Drizzle each sandwich with remaining yogurt mixture. Top with onion and cheese. Serve immediately or broil until cheese melts, about 2 minutes. Garnish with fresh greens or basil, if desired.

Makes 4 to 5 servings

helpful hint

Avocados are picked unripe and are often found unripe in the supermarket too. If you plan on using them right away, look for specimens that yield to gentle pressure. However, they should not feel soft or mushy. If the flesh has shrunken away from the peel, they are overripe and should be avoided. Firm avocados will eventually ripen but avoid those that are rock-hard.

FISH & SHELLFISH ESSENTIALS

Cooking fish and shellfish may seem intimidating to a first-time cook, however, it can be quite simple. Learning some basic information about buying, storing and cooking fish and shellfish will help the cooking process go much smoother. Fish is very versatile, delicious and nutritious. It also cooks quickly—once you learn how long to cook it you'll be on your way to many wonderful meals. Many shellfish can be found in the supermarket seafood case—lobster, shrimp, scallops, clams, mussels, oysters and octopus. Try some of the following recipes and you'll soon feel like a master at cooking seafood.

CUTS OF FISH: Fish come in various forms. The most readily available forms of fish are whole, dressed, pan-dressed, fillet and steaks. Fillets and steaks are a good choice for inexperienced cooks.

BUYING TIPS FOR FISH

•It is important to know what to look for when purchasing fresh fish. One can find fresh fish at most large supermarkets or at a retail fish market.

•When buying whole fish, look for bright, clear and protruding eyes rather than dull, hazy sunken ones. The skin should be moist and shiny, the gills red or pink and the flesh firm and elastic. A fresh fish should have a mild, slightly oceanlike odor rather than a fishy or sour smell.

•Fish fillets and steaks should have moist flesh that is free from discoloration and skin that is shiny and resilient. Again, if the fillet or steak has a strong odor, it is not fresh.

•Frozen fish should have its original shape with the wrapper intact. Do not allow frozen fish to thaw on the way home from the store.

STORING FISH: When storing fresh fish, wrap it tightly in plastic wrap. If possible, place the package on ice and store in the coldest part of the refrigerator. Be sure that melting ice drains away from the fish. If the flesh comes in contact with moisture, it may become discolored. Fresh fish should be used within a day.

COOKING METHODS OF FISH

The most common methods of cooking fish are pan frying, deep-frying, sautéing, poaching, broiling, grilling, baking and microwaving. Before cooking, rinse fish under cold running water and pat dry with paper towels. Fish cooks quickly. Be careful not to overcook it as this makes the fish tough and destroys flavor. Cooking times vary with each fish and cut. For grilling or broiling fish, a good guidline is to cook 10 minutes per inch of fish.

BUYING TIPS FOR SHELLFISH

All fresh shellfish should have a mild aroma and smell of the sea. Avoid shellfish that have a strong fishy odor. Fresh shellfish are very perishable. If you are in doubt about the freshness of any shellfish, do not buy it. If you are purchasing live shellfish, it is best to buy them as close to the time you plan to cook them as possible. Fresh shellfish should be cooked on the day they are purchased. Frozen shellfish should be packaged in a close-fitting moisture-proof package that is intact at the time of purchase.

STORING SEAFOOD

Shellfish are highly perishable and it is best to use them within 24 hours of purchase. They need to be handled carefully before cooking to keep them fresh or alive. The most important factor is to keep them in a cold, moist environment. Keep fresh or thawed shellfish as close to 32°F as possible. Store shrimp and shucked shellfish in a leakproof bag or covered container in the refrigerator. Store live shellfish in a shallow dish covered with a damp towel. If available, you may also want to keep the shellfish covered with seaweed. Frozen shellfish can be stored in the freezer for three to six months. The longer it is stored, the greater the loss of flavor, texture and moisture.

TESTING FISH AND SHELLFISH FOR DONENESS

Most shellfish take very few minutes to cook and it is very important not to overcook them. If shellfish are cooked too long, they become tough and dry and lose much of their flavor. Heat precooked shellfish just to the desired temperature. Follow these guidelines for specific doneness tests:

Clams   until clams open

Fish   until fish begins to flake when tested with a fork

Shrimp   until shrimp are pink and opaque

Scallops   until scallops are opaque

NO-FUSS FISH & SHELLFISH

penne with shrimp and vegetables

2 tablespoons olive or vegetable oil

2 medium zucchini, cut into 2-inch strips (about 2 cups)

1 tablespoon minced shallots

8 ounces medium shrimp, peeled, deveined

1 medium yellow bell pepper, cut into 2-inch strips (about 1 cup)

1 can (14.5-ounce can) CONTADINA® Recipe Ready Diced Tomatoes with Roasted Garlic, undrained

1 cup sliced pitted ripe olives, drained

1 tablespoon capers

8 ounces dry penne pasta, cooked, drained, kept warm

1. Heat oil in large skillet. Add zucchini and shallots; sauté 1 to 2 minutes or until zucchini are crisp-tender.

2. Add shrimp and bell pepper; sauté 2 to 4 minutes or until shrimp turn pink.

3. Stir in undrained tomatoes, olives and capers; simmer, uncovered, 2 minutes. Serve over pasta.

Makes 6 servings

helpful hint

To devein shrimp, make a small cut along the back and lift out the dark vein with the tip of a knife. You may find the task easier if it is done under cold running water. There are also special gadgets available that make peeling and deveining shrimp a one-step process.

penne with shrimp and vegetables

NO-FUSS FISH & SHELLFISH

cheesy tuna pie

2 cups cooked rice

2 cans (6 ounces each) tuna, drained and flaked

1 cup mayonnaise

1 cup (4 ounces) shredded Cheddar cheese

½ cup sour cream

½ cup thinly sliced celery

1 can (4 ounces) sliced black olives

2 tablespoons onion flakes

1 refrigerated pie crust

1. Preheat oven to 350°F. Spray 9-inch, deep-dish pie pan with nonstick cooking spray.

2. Combine all ingredients except pie crust in medium bowl; mix well. Spoon into prepared pie pan. Place pie crust over tuna mixture; press edge to pie pan to seal. Cut slits for steam to escape.

3. Bake 20 minutes or until crust is browned and filling is bubbly.   *Makes 6 servings*

helpful hint

Canned tuna is precooked and is packed in either water or oil. It is available in various quality grades—fancy, containing large pieces of meat; chunk, with smaller pieces; and flake, which contains even smaller bits and pieces.

grilled garlic-pepper shrimp

⅓ cup olive oil

2 tablespoons lemon juice

1 teaspoon garlic pepper blend

20 jumbo shrimp, peeled and deveined

Lemon wedges (optional)

1. Prepare grill for direct grilling.

2. Meanwhile, combine oil, lemon juice and garlic pepper in large resealable plastic food storage bag; add shrimp. Marinate 30 minutes in refrigerator, turning bag once.

3. Thread 5 shrimp onto each of 4 skewers; reserve marinade. Grill on grid over medium heat 6 minutes or until pink and opaque, turning and brushing with marinade after 3 minutes. Serve with lemon wedges, if desired.   *Makes 4 servings*

cheesy tuna pie

tuna pot pie

1 tablespoon butter

1 small onion, chopped

1 can (10¾ ounces) condensed cream of potato soup

¼ cup milk

½ teaspoon dried thyme leaves

¼ teaspoon salt

⅛ teaspoon black pepper

2 cans (6 ounces each) albacore tuna in water, drained

1 package (16 ounces) frozen vegetable medley, such as broccoli, green beans, carrots and red peppers, thawed

2 tablespoons chopped fresh parsley

1 can (8 ounces) refrigerated crescent roll dough

1. Preheat oven to 350°F. Spray 11×7-inch baking dish with nonstick cooking spray.

2. Melt butter in large skillet over medium heat. Add onion; cook and stir 2 minutes or until onion is tender. Add soup, milk, thyme, salt and pepper; cook and stir 3 to 4 minutes or until thick and bubbly. Stir in tuna, vegetables and parsley. Pour mixture into prepared dish.

3. Unroll crescent roll dough and divide into triangles. Place triangles over tuna filling without overlapping dough. Bake, uncovered, 20 minutes or until triangles are golden brown. Let stand 5 minutes before serving.

Makes 6 servings

Tip: Experiment with different vegetable combinations and create an exciting recipe every time. Just substitute a new medley for the one listed and enjoy the results.

tuna pot pie

marinated salmon with lemon tarragon sauce

¼ **cup lemon juice**

¼ **cup olive oil**

 2 **cloves garlic, crushed**

½ **teaspoon salt**

¼ **teaspoon black pepper**

 1 **pound fresh
   1-inch-thick salmon
   fillet**

⅔ **cup sour cream**

¼ **cup minced green
   onions**

¼ **cup milk**

 1 **tablespoon fresh
   tarragon leaves *or*
   1 teaspoon dried
   tarragon leaves**

¼ **teaspoon salt**

Combine lemon juice, olive oil, garlic, salt and pepper in shallow, nonreactive 11×7-inch baking dish. Mix well. Add salmon; turn twice to coat with marinade. With salmon skin-side up in baking dish, cover tightly and refrigerate 2 hours. Combine remaining ingredients in small bowl; mix well. Cover and refrigerate until ready to serve.

Cut salmon into 4 pieces. Preheat grill or broiler. If grilling, cook over medium-hot coals 5 minutes per side or until fish begins to flake when tested with fork. If broiling, place skin side down on broiling pan. Cook 6 inches from heat 8 to 10 minutes or until fish just begins to flake when tested with fork. Serve hot with chilled sauce spooned over each piece.

Makes 4 servings

marinated salmon with lemon
tarragon sauce

tuna monte cristo sandwiches

4 thin slices (2 ounces)
  Cheddar cheese

4 oval slices sourdough
  or challah (egg)
  bread

½ pound deli tuna salad

1 egg, beaten

¼ cup milk

2 tablespoons butter or
  margarine

1. Place 1 slice cheese on each bread slice. Spread tuna salad evenly over two slices of cheese-topped bread. Close sandwich with remaining bread.

2. Combine egg and milk in shallow bowl. Dip sandwiches in egg mixture, turning to coat well.

3. Melt butter in large nonstick skillet over medium heat. Add sandwiches; cook 4 to 5 minutes per side or until golden brown and cheese is melted.

Makes 2 servings

Serving suggestion: Serve with a chilled fruit salad.

Prep and Cook Time: 20 minutes

cajun shrimp wraps

½ cup uncooked rice

1 tablespoon olive oil

1 pound uncooked
  medium shrimp,
  peeled and deveined

1 small red onion,
  chopped

1 tablespoon finely
  chopped garlic

2 teaspoons Cajun
  seasoning (optional)

1 cup RAGÚ® Old World
  Style® Pasta Sauce

8 (8-inch) flour tortillas,
  warmed

Cook rice according to package directions.

Meanwhile, in 12-inch skillet, heat olive oil over medium-high heat and cook shrimp, onion, garlic and Cajun seasoning 3 minutes or until shrimp turn pink. Stir in Ragú Old World Style Pasta Sauce; heat through. Stir hot cooked rice into shrimp mixture. Spoon ½ cup filling onto each tortilla; roll and serve.

Makes 8 servings

Recipe Tip: To peel and devein shrimp, start at the head of the shrimp and use your fingers to peel off the shell. Use a sharp knife to slit the back and lift out the dark vein.

tuna monte cristo sandwich

shrimp and vegetables with lo mein noodles

2 tablespoons vegetable oil

1 pound uncooked medium shrimp, peeled

2 packages (21 ounces each) frozen lo mein stir-fry mix with sauce

2 tablespoons fresh chopped cilantro

1 small wedge cabbage

¼ cup peanuts, chopped

1. Heat oil in wok or large skillet over medium-high heat. Add shrimp; stir-fry 3 minutes or until shrimp are pink and opaque. Remove shrimp from wok to medium bowl. Set aside.

2. Remove sauce packet from stir-fry mix. Add frozen vegetables and noodles to wok; stir in sauce. Cover and cook 7 to 8 minutes, stirring frequently.

3. While vegetable mixture is cooking, shred cabbage.

4. Stir shrimp, cilantro and peanuts into vegetable mixture; heat through. Serve immediately with cabbage. *Makes 6 servings*

Prep and Cook Time: 20 minutes

helpful hint

Since medium shrimp do not require deveining, substitute them for large shrimp whenever possible to save valuable preparation time.

shrimp and vegetables
with lo mein noodles

sizzling florida shrimp

1½ pounds Florida Shrimp, peeled and deveined

1 cup Florida mushrooms, cut in halves

½ cup Florida red bell pepper pieces (1-inch pieces)

½ cup Florida onion pieces (1-inch pieces)

1 (8.9-ounce) jar Flavor Medleys™ Lemon Pepper Sauce

helpful hint

Soak wooden skewers in water for about 30 minutes before using to prevent burning.

Arrange shrimp on wooden skewers with mushrooms, red bell pepper and onion. Place skewers in a glass dish and cover with sauce, reserving about 2 tablespoons for basting during cooking. Cover dish and refrigerate for 1 hour. Prepare grill surface by cleaning and coating with oil. Coals are ready when they are no longer flaming but are covered with gray ash. Place skewers on grill about 6 inches from the coals. Let shrimp grill for about 3 to 4 minutes on each side, basting before turning once. Serve with sautéed asparagus and grilled garlic bread. *Makes 4 servings*

*Favorite recipe from **Florida Department of Agriculture and Consumer Services, Bureau of Seafood and Aquaculture***

sizzling florida shrimp

pasta with red clam sauce

1 tablespoon vegetable oil

2 cans (6½ ounces each) chopped clams, drained and rinsed

1 jar (26 ounces) chunky marinara or tomato sauce

1 package (9 ounces) frozen green peas

1 pound whole wheat or white linguine, cooked al dente

1. In a 2½ quart pan, over medium heat, combine oil and clams. Heat, stirring, until clams begin to sizzle, about 5 minutes.

2. Add marinara sauce. Bring to a boil; reduce heat, simmer until slightly reduced, about 15 to 20 minutes.

3. Add frozen peas and heat, stirring, until peas are cooked through, about 5 minutes.

4. To serve, divide pasta equally among 6 bowls and ladle sauce on top.   *Makes 6 servings*

chile 'n lime shrimp

⅓ cup *Frank's® RedHot®* **Chile 'n Lime™ Hot Sauce**

2 tablespoons olive oil

1 teaspoon minced garlic

1 pound large shrimp, shelled and deveined

1 cup chopped green, red or yellow bell pepper

½ cup chopped red onion

HEAT **Chile 'n Lime**™ Hot Sauce, oil and garlic in medium skillet. Cook over high heat until sauce is bubbly, stirring often.

ADD shrimp, bell pepper and onion. Cook, stirring, 3 to 5 minutes until shrimp are pink and coated with sauce. Serve with rice, if desired.   *Makes 3 to 4 servings*

Prep Time: 5 minutes
Cook Time: 6 minutes

maryland crab cakes

1 pound fresh backfin crabmeat, cartilage removed

10 reduced-sodium crackers (2 inches each), crushed to equal ½ cup crumbs

1 rib celery, finely chopped

1 green onion, finely chopped

¼ cup cholesterol-free egg substitute

3 tablespoons fat-free tartar sauce

1 teaspoon seafood seasoning

2 teaspoons vegetable oil

1. Combine crabmeat, cracker crumbs, celery and onion in medium bowl; set aside.

2. Mix egg substitute, tartar sauce and seafood seasoning in small bowl; pour over crabmeat mixture. Gently mix so large lumps will not be broken. Shape into 6 (¾-inch-thick) patties. Cover; refrigerate 30 minutes.

3. Spray large skillet with nonstick cooking spray. Add oil; heat over medium-high heat. Place crab cakes in skillet; cook 3 to 4 minutes on each side or until cakes are lightly browned. Garnish with lemon wedges or slices, if desired. *Makes 6 servings*

helpful hint

Whole crabs and crabmeat should smell sweet, not fishy.

maryland crab cakes

salmon with warm mango salsa

1¼ pounds salmon fillet, about 1 inch thick

½ teaspoon paprika

⅛ teaspoon ground red pepper

4 sheets (18×12 inches) heavy-duty foil, lightly sprayed with nonstick cooking spray

2 medium mangoes, peeled, seeded and cut into ¾-inch pieces

½ medium red bell pepper, chopped

1 jalapeño pepper,* seeded and finely chopped

2 tablespoons chopped fresh parsley

1 tablespoon frozen orange-pineapple juice concentrate or orange juice concentrate, thawed

*Jalapeño peppers can sting and irritate the skin; wear rubber gloves when handling peppers and do not touch eyes. Wash hands after handling.

1. Prepare grill for direct cooking.

2. Rinse salmon under cold running water; pat dry with paper towels. Cut salmon into 4 serving-size pieces. Place one piece salmon, skin side down, on each sheet of foil. Combine paprika and red pepper in small bowl. Rub on tops of salmon pieces.

3. Toss together mangoes, bell pepper, jalapeño pepper, parsley and juice concentrate. Spoon onto salmon pieces.

4. Double-fold sides and ends of foil to seal packets, leaving head space for heat circulation. Place on baking sheet.

5. Slide packets off baking sheet onto grill grid. Grill, covered, over medium-high coals 9 to 11 minutes or until fish flakes when tested with fork. Carefully open one end of each packet to allow steam to escape. Open packets and transfer to serving plates.

Makes 4 servings

salmon with warm mango salsa

cajun catfish with red beans and rice

Red Beans and Rice
(recipe follows,
optional)

6 skinless catfish fillets
(6 ounces each)

12 frozen deveined
shelled large
shrimp, thawed

⅓ cup olive oil

1 teaspoon dried thyme
leaves

1 teaspoon dried
oregano leaves

2 cloves garlic, minced

½ teaspoon salt

½ teaspoon black pepper

⅛ to ¼ teaspoon ground
red pepper

6 sheets (15×12 inches)
heavy-duty foil,
lightly sprayed with
nonstick cooking
spray

1. Preheat oven to 450°F. Prepare Red Beans and Rice, if desired.

2. Place catfish and shrimp in resealable plastic food storage bag. Combine oil, thyme, oregano, garlic, salt, black pepper and red pepper in small bowl. Add to bag. Seal bag; turn bag to coat fish and shrimp. Marinate 30 minutes.

3. Remove fish and shrimp from marinade; discard remaining marinade. Place one fish fillet in center of 1 foil sheet. Top with 2 shrimp.

4. Double fold sides and ends of foil to seal packet, leaving head space for heat circulation. Repeat with remaining fish, shrimp and foil sheets to make 5 more packets. Place packets on baking sheet.

5. Bake 25 minutes. Let stand 5 minutes. Open packet and transfer contents to serving plates. Serve with Red Beans and Rice. *Makes 6 servings*

cajun catfish with red beans and rice

helpful hint

For a milder flavor, reduce the chili powder to 2 teaspoons.

red beans and rice

1 cup water

½ cup uncooked rice

½ teaspoon salt

1 can (15 ounces) kidney beans, rinsed and drained

1 can (14½ ounces) diced tomatoes, undrained

2 tablespoons bacon bits

1 tablespoon chili powder

1 large heavy-duty foil baking bag (17×15 inches), lightly sprayed with nonstick cooking spray

1. Preheat oven to 450°F.

2. Place water, rice and salt in 2-quart microwavable container; microwave at HIGH 7 minutes.

3. Add remaining ingredients, except foil bag; stir until blended. Place foil bag in 1-inch deep jelly-roll pan; spoon rice mixture into bag. Double fold bag to seal. Shake baking pan to distribute contents of bag evenly.

4. Bake 45 minutes. Let stand 5 minutes. Carefully cut bag open. Fold back top to allow steam to escape; serve.

Makes 6 (1-cup) servings

tuna salad pita pockets

1 (9-ounce) can tuna, drained

1 cup chopped cucumber

¼ cup part-skim ricotta cheese

2 tablespoons reduced-fat mayonnaise

2 tablespoons red wine vinegar

2 green onions, chopped

1 tablespoon sweet pickle relish

2 cloves garlic, finely chopped

½ teaspoon salt

¼ teaspoon black pepper

1 cup alfalfa sprouts

2 pita breads, halved

Combine all ingredients except sprouts and bread. Fill bread with sprouts and tuna mixture.

Makes 4 servings

tuna salad pita pocket

broiled shrimp kabobs

2 tablespoons olive oil

2 tablespoons lemon juice

½ teaspoon bottled minced garlic

½ teaspoon salt

½ teaspoon dried oregano leaves

⅛ teaspoon ground red pepper

½ pound uncooked medium shrimp, peeled

1 red bell pepper, cut into squares

1 medium zucchini, cut into ½-inch slices

1. Preheat broiler. Whisk together oil, lemon juice, garlic, salt, oregano and ground red pepper in medium bowl. Add shrimp, bell pepper and zucchini; stir until well coated.

2. Alternately thread shrimp, bell pepper and zucchini onto skewers. Place on rack of broiler pan. Broil 4 inches from heat 2 minutes per side or until shrimp turn pink and opaque. *Makes 4 servings*

Prep and Cook Time: 20 minutes

poached salmon & asparagus

2 tablespoons butter

1 cup onion, sliced

2 stalks celery, sliced

1 cup asparagus stems, sliced

2 packages UNCLE BEN'S NATURAL SELECT® Garlic & Butter Flavor Rice

3 cups water

6 pieces salmon fillets

1 cup asparagus tips

1. In large skillet with tight-fitting lid, melt butter over medium heat and sauté onion, celery and asparagus stems for about 3 minutes.

2. Add rice and water; bring to a boil. Carefully place fillets on top of rice; reduce heat. Cover and simmer about 4 minutes.

3. Arrange asparagus tips around salmon fillets; cover and simmer 6 to 8 minutes longer. *Makes 6 servings*

Preparation Time: 10 minutes

tempting tuna parmesano

2 large cloves garlic

1 package (9 ounces) refrigerated fresh angel hair pasta

¼ cup butter or margarine

1 cup whipping cream

1 cup frozen peas

¼ teaspoon salt

1 can (6 ounces) white tuna in water, drained

¼ cup grated Parmesan cheese, plus additional for serving

Black pepper

1. Fill large deep skillet ¾ full with water. Cover and bring to a boil over high heat. Meanwhile, peel and mince garlic.

2. Add pasta to skillet; boil 1 to 2 minutes or until pasta is al dente. Do not overcook. Drain; set aside.

3. Add butter and garlic to skillet; cook over medium-high heat until butter is melted and sizzling. Stir in cream, peas and salt; bring to a boil.

4. Break tuna into chunks and stir into skillet with ¼ cup cheese. Return pasta to skillet. Cook until heated through; toss gently. Serve with additional cheese and pepper to taste. *Makes 2 to 3 servings*

Serving Suggestion: Serve with a tossed romaine and tomato salad with Italian dressing.

Prep and Cook Time: 16 minutes

tempting tuna parmesano

nutty pan-fried trout

2 tablespoons oil

4 trout fillets (about 6 ounces each)

½ cup seasoned bread crumbs

½ cup pine nuts

helpful hint

Fish fillets and steaks should have moist flesh that is free from discoloration and skin that is shiny and resilient. Again, if the fillet or steak has a strong odor, it is not fresh.

1. Heat oil in large skillet over medium heat. Lightly coat fish with crumbs. Add to skillet.

2. Cook 8 minutes or until fish flakes easily when tested with fork, turning after 5 minutes. Remove fish from skillet. Place on serving platter; keep warm.

3. Add nuts to drippings in skillet. Cook and stir 3 minutes or until nuts are lightly toasted. Sprinkle over fish. *Makes 4 servings*

nutty pan-fried trout

boiled whole lobster with burned butter sauce

Burned Butter Sauce

- **½ cup (1 stick) butter**
- **2 tablespoons chopped fresh parsley**
- **1 tablespoon capers**
- **1 tablespoon cider vinegar**
- **2 live lobsters**

helpful hint

Purchase live lobsters as close to time of cooking as possible. Store in refrigerator until ready to cook.

Fill 8-quart stockpot with enough water to cover lobsters. Cover stockpot; bring water to a boil over high heat. Meanwhile, to make Burned Butter Sauce, melt butter in medium saucepan over medium heat. Cook and stir butter until it turns dark chocolate brown. Remove from heat. Add parsley, capers and vinegar. Pour into 2 individual ramekins; set aside.

Holding each lobster by its back, submerge head first into boiling water. Cover and continue to heat. When water returns to a boil, cook lobsters for 10 to 18 minutes, depending on size:1 pound—10 minutes; 1¼ pounds—12 minutes; 1½ pounds—15 minutes; 2 pounds—18 minutes.

Transfer to 2 large serving platters. Remove bands restraining claws. Cut through underside of shells with kitchen shears and loosen meat from shells. Provide nutcrackers and seafood forks. Serve lobsters with Burned Butter Sauce. *Makes 2 servings*

snappy halibut skillet

½ teaspoon thyme, crushed

1½ pounds halibut or other firm white fish

1 tablespoon olive oil

1 onion, chopped

1 clove garlic, minced

1 tablespoon cornstarch

1 can (14½ ounces) DEL MONTE® Stewed Tomatoes, No Salt Added

¼ cup sliced green onions

1. Sprinkle thyme over both sides of fish. In large skillet, cook fish in hot oil over medium-high heat until fish flakes easily when tested with fork. Remove fish to plate; keep warm.

2. Cook chopped onion and garlic in same skillet until tender. Stir cornstarch into tomatoes; pour into skillet. Cook, stirring frequently, until thickened. Return fish to skillet; top with green onions. Heat through.

Makes 4 servings

helpful hint

When storing fresh fish, wrap it tightly in plastic wrap. If possible, place the package on ice and store it in the coldest part of the refrigerator. Be sure that melting ice drains away from the fish. If the flesh comes in contact with moisture, it may become discolored. Fresh fish should be used within a day.

snappy halibut skillet

caribbean chicken & shrimp skewers

1 cup LAWRY'S®
    Caribbean Jerk
    Marinade With
    Papaya Juice,
    divided

1 pound boneless,
    skinless chicken
    breasts, cut into
    chunks

    Wooden skewers

15 medium shrimp,
    peeled and deveined

1 red bell pepper, cut
    into ½-inch pieces

1 can (20 ounces)
    pineapple chunks,
    drained

In large resealable plastic bag, combine ⅔ cup Caribbean Jerk Marinade and chicken; seal bag and shake to coat. Marinate in refrigerator for at least 30 minutes. Remove chicken from bag, discarding used marinade. On wooden skewers, thread chicken, shrimp, red peppers and pineapple. Grill or broil until chicken is thoroughly cooked, turning once and brushing often with remaining ⅓ cup Marinade, about 8 to 12 minutes.

Makes 15 skewers

Variations: For variety, try Lawry's® Hawaiian Marinade With Tropical Juices or Lawry's® Teriyaki Marinade With Pineapple Juice instead of Caribbean Jerk Marinade.

Hint: Soak wooden skewers in water for about 30 minutes before using to help reduce burning.

Prep. Time: 15 minutes
Marinating Time: 30 minutes
Cook Time: 8 to 12 minutes

chicken hollandaise with asparagus and crabmeat

½ cup prepared Hollandaise sauce

½ teaspoon seafood seasoning

¼ cup fresh chives, chopped

1 tablespoon flour

Salt and pepper, to taste

½ (16-ounce) package PERDUE® Fit 'N Easy® Thin-Sliced Skinless & Boneless Chicken Breast or Turkey Breast Cutlets (8 ounces)

1 tablespoon butter

4 ounces jumbo lump crabmeat

8 asparagus spears, steamed

4 lemon wedges

Whisk together Hollandaise sauce, seafood seasoning and 3 tablespoons chives in a small bowl.

In a shallow dish, stir together flour, salt and pepper. Coat chicken slices on both sides with flour. Melt butter in a large, non-stick skillet over high heat. Add chicken and sauté until brown on both sides and firm.

Reduce heat to low; add crabmeat and ¼ cup Hollandaise to skillet. Stir gently until warm.

To serve, divide chicken between 2 plates. Top with asparagus and crabmeat. Spoon remaining Hollandaise over and sprinkle with remaining chives. Garnish with lemon wedges.   *Makes 2 servings*

Prep Time: 20 minutes
Cook Time: 5 minutes

helpful hint

Choose fresh-looking asparagus stalks with closed, compact tips. Open tips are a sign of over-maturity. At home, keep asparagus cold and humid. Use it quickly to enjoy the best fresh flavor and texture.

bow tie pasta with smoked salmon lemon sauce

½ cup CRISCO® Pure Canola Oil

4 to 6 cloves garlic, finely chopped

½ cup chopped onion

1 pound bow tie pasta

3 tablespoons fresh lemon juice

½ cup chopped scallions

¼ cup chopped Italian parsley (plus more for garnish)

½ pound sliced smoked salmon slices

Salt and pepper

Thin lemon slices for garnish

Heat the CRISCO® Pure Canola Oil in a skillet over low heat; add the garlic and onion. Cook until the garlic and onion are soft. Set aside.

Cook the bow tie pasta and drain well. Put the pasta back in the pot it was cooked in. Add the garlic and onion mixture and mix well. Add the lemon juice, scallions, parsley, and salmon, and mix well again.

Season with salt and pepper to taste. Garnish with Italian parsley and lemon slices, if desired.

Makes 4 to 6 servings

helpful hint

Although salmon has a higher fat content than most fish, it is still very nutritious. Salmon's fat content is made up primarily of omega-3 fatty acids. There is a wealth of research available today that links consumption of omega-3 fatty acids with the reduced risk of heart attack and heart disease.

shrimp bourgeois

1 package UNCLE BEN'S® Long Grain & Wild Rice Original Recipe

2 tablespoons butter

¼ cup pecan halves

1 pound raw shrimp, peeled, leaving the tails

1 cup mushrooms, thickly sliced

8 cherry tomatoes, quartered

1. Cook rice according to package directions.

2. When rice is almost ready, melt butter in a skillet and gently toast the pecan halves. Remove from pan, leaving the butter.

3. Reheat pan, add shrimp and brown on one side. Turn shrimp over and push them to the sides of pan.

4. Place mushrooms in the middle of pan and allow to gently soften.

5. Mix rice into pan with the shrimp and mushrooms.

6. Stir in pecans and tomatoes.   *Makes 3 servings*

Preparation Time: 15 minutes

orange scallops with spinach and walnuts

12 sea scallops (approximately ¾ pound)

½ cup freshly squeezed orange juice

2 tablespoons olive oil

2 packages (8 ounces each) fresh baby spinach, washed and stemmed

2 tablespoons toasted walnuts

Salt and white pepper to taste

4 orange wedges

1. Rinse sea scallops and slice in half horizontally. Place in nonreactive dish and add orange juice. Stir well and set aside.

2. Place a 12-inch skillet over medium heat and add oil. Add spinach and cook until heated through and just wilted, stirring often.

3. Push spinach to edges of pan, forming a ring. Increase heat to medium high. Place scallops in the center of pan and cook scallops 1 to 2 minutes, turning once.

4. Add walnuts and season with salt and white pepper. To serve, make a bed of spinach on the plate; top with scallops and pan juices. Serve with orange wedge on the side.   *Makes 4 servings*

halibut with roasted pepper sauce

Roasted Pepper Sauce (recipe follows)

1 medium onion, thinly sliced

1 large clove garlic, minced

1 (1½-pound) halibut fillet, skinned

Preheat oven to 425°F. Grease shallow baking dish. Prepare Roasted Pepper Sauce; set aside. Cover bottom of baking dish with onion and garlic. Top with fish and sauce. Bake 20 minutes or until fish flakes easily when tested with fork. Garnish as desired.

Makes 4 servings

roasted pepper sauce

1 (7-ounce) can chopped green chilies, drained

1 (7-ounce) jar roasted red peppers, drained

⅔ cup chicken broth

Combine ingredients in food processor or blender; process until smooth.

vermouth salmon

2 (10×10-inch) sheets heavy-duty foil

2 salmon fillets or steaks (3 ounces each)

Pinch of salt and black pepper

4 sprigs fresh dill

2 slices lemon

1 tablespoon vermouth

1. Preheat oven to 375°F. Turn up edges of 1 sheet of foil so juices will not run out. Place salmon in center of foil. Sprinkle with salt and pepper. Place dill and lemon slices on top of salmon. Pour vermouth evenly over fish pieces.

2. Cover fish with second sheet of foil. Crimp edges of foil together to seal packet, leaving head space for heat circulation. Place packet on baking sheet. Bake 20 to 25 minutes or until salmon flakes easily when tested with fork.

Makes 2 servings

clockwise from top: lemony steamed broccoli (page 242), halibut with roasted pepper sauce and oven-roasted potatoes (page 245)

tuna-macaroni casserole

1 cup mayonnaise

1 cup (4 ounces) shredded Swiss cheese

½ cup milk

¼ cup chopped onion

¼ cup chopped sweet red bell pepper or pimiento

⅛ teaspoon black pepper

2 cans (7 ounces each) tuna, drained and flaked

1 package (about 10 ounces) frozen peas

2 cups shell pasta or elbow macaroni, cooked and drained

½ cup dry bread crumbs (optional)

2 tablespoons melted butter or corn oil (optional)

1. Preheat oven to 350°F.

2. Stir together mayonnaise, cheese, milk, onion, bell pepper and black pepper in large bowl. Add tuna, peas and macaroni, toss to coat well.

3. Spoon into 2-quart casserole. If desired, mix bread crumbs with butter in small bowl and sprinkle over top. Bake 30 to 40 minutes or until heated through.

Makes 6 servings

helpful hint

The next time you're making a casserole, assemble and bake two. Allow one to cool completely, then wrap it in heavy-duty foil and freeze it for another day. To reheat a frozen 2-quart casserole, unwrap it and microwave, covered, at HIGH for 20 to 30 minutes, stirring once or twice during cooking. Allow to stand about 5 minutes.

grilled glazed salmon

⅓ cup apple juice

2 tablespoons soy sauce

½ teaspoon minced gingerroot

⅛ teaspoon black pepper

1¼ pounds salmon fillet

1. Prepare grill for direct cooking. Combine apple juice, soy sauce, gingerroot and pepper in small saucepan. Bring to a boil over medium heat. Reduce heat; simmer apple juice mixture about 10 minutes or until syrupy. Cool slightly.

2. Brush side of salmon fillet without skin with apple juice mixture. Grill salmon, flesh side down, on oiled grid over medium-hot heat 5 minutes. Turn and brush salmon with apple mixture. Grill 5 more minutes or until fish flakes easily when tested with fork.

Makes 4 servings

fettuccine with shrimp in light tomato sauce

1 tablespoon olive oil

1 pound medium shrimp, peeled and deveined

3 cloves garlic, finely chopped

1 jar (1 pound 10 ounces) RAGÚ® Light Pasta Sauce

⅛ teaspoon red pepper flakes

1 package (12 ounces) fettuccine, cooked and drained

2 tablespoon grated Parmesan cheese

In 10-inch skillet, heat olive oil over medium heat and cook shrimp and garlic 3 minutes or until shrimp are almost pink. Stir in RAGÚ Light Pasta Sauce and red pepper flakes. Simmer uncovered, stirring occasionally, 2 minutes or until shrimp turn pink and sauce is heated through. Spoon sauce and shrimp over hot fettuccine and sprinkle with cheese. Garnish, if desired, with finely chopped fresh parsley.

Makes 6 servings

LOW-FAT LEARNING

Eating is one of life's greatest pleasures. What better feeling is there than the one you get when you sink your teeth into a bit of dark, rich, chocolate-fudge cake or into a thick juicy grilled-to-perfection burger? Your whole body feels contentment. And yet all we do is try to keep ourselves from these "bad" foods—whether we're trying to lose weight or just want to stay healthy. It's hard to withstand the urge for these pleasures though. We need to change the way we think about food. There are no "bad" foods. All edible foods can be included in a healthy meal plan. The key is moderation.

Things to keep in mind when trying to maintain a healthy lifestyle:

•When trying to lose weight, many people try decreasing the amount of fat they consume. Some fat is necessary for good health, but you need to be aware of the types of fats you're consuming. Saturated fats, found most often in foods of animal origin, are the most unhealthy of the fats and should be eaten in limited amounts. Other fats, such as the ones found in fish and whole grains, have been shown to have health-protective benefits.

•Eating between 21 and 38 grams of fiber each day is helpful in preventing certain types of cancer as well as protecting the heart from many diseases. Fiber comes in a variety of plant-based foods—fruits, vegetables and whole grains. Fiber also gives you the feeling of fullness more than other foods do. This will allow you to eat less during your meals.

•Water is a necessity for life. Try drinking between eight and ten (8-ounce) cups per day. Drinking water is another good way to fill up.

•Too much sodium is a problem in many people's diets. Try using low-sodium versions of well-known foods or using herbs and spices instead of salt in your diet.

Cooking Healthier

When cooking great-tasting low-fat meals, you will find some techniques or ingredients are different from traditional cooking. Fat, in the form of oil, butter, margarine and shortening is used in nearly every type of recipe. Because fat plays an important role in cooking and baking, it is difficult to merely omit it. It acts as a flavor enhancer and gives food a distinctive and desirable texture. So, instead of taking it out completely, several techniques are employed to make up for the loss of flavor and texture. These techniques include:

•Investing in nonstick bakeware and using nonstick cooking spray to reduce the need for added oil.

•Incorporating applesauce or other puréed fruit into baked goods to replace some of the fat. This helps to create a texture similar to higher-fat foods.

•"Sautéing" vegetables in a small amount of broth to further reduce the need for oil.

•Using herbs, spices and flavorful vegetables in a variety of combinations to highlight the natural flavor of food, making up for the lack of fat.

•Choosing alternative protein sources, such as dried beans or tofu in recipes. Often, meat is included in recipes as an accent flavor rather than the staring attraction.

These methods for reducing fat can benefit recipes in two ways:

1) by reducing the overall amount of fat in the recipes and

2) by boosting the nutritional content of the recipes when fruits and vegetables replace high-fat ingredients.

These are all simple changes that you can easily make when you start cooking light and healthy!

LIGHT DINING

caribbean sea bass with mango salsa

4 skinless sea bass fillets
   (4 ounces each),
   about 1 inch thick

1 teaspoon Caribbean
   jerk seasoning

   Nonstick cooking
   spray

1 ripe mango, peeled,
   pitted and diced, *or*
   1 cup diced drained
   bottled mango

2 tablespoons chopped
   fresh cilantro

2 teaspoons fresh lime
   juice

1 teaspoon minced fresh
   or bottled jalapeño
   pepper*

*Jalapeño peppers can sting and
irritate the skin; wear rubber gloves
when handling peppers and do not
touch eyes. Wash hands after
handling.*

1. Prepare grill or preheat broiler. Sprinkle fish with seasoning; coat lightly with cooking spray. Grill fish over medium coals or broil 5 inches from heat 4 to 5 minutes per side or until fish flakes easily when tested with fork.

2. Meanwhile, combine mango, cilantro, lime juice and jalapeño pepper in small bowl; mix well. Serve salsa over fish. *Makes 4 servings*

Prep Time: 10 minutes
Cook Time: 8 minutes

caribbean sea bass with
mango salsa

saucy broccoli and spaghetti

3 ounces uncooked
spaghetti

1 package (10 ounces)
frozen chopped
broccoli

½ cup thinly sliced leek,
white part only

½ cup fat-free (skim)
milk

2 teaspoons cornstarch

2 teaspoons chopped
fresh oregano *or*
½ teaspoon dried
oregano leaves

⅛ teaspoon hot pepper
sauce

3 tablespoons reduced-
fat cream cheese,
softened

1 tablespoon grated
Romano or
Parmesan cheese

1 tablespoon chopped
fresh parsley

1. Prepare spaghetti according to package directions, omitting salt; drain and keep warm. Meanwhile, cook broccoli and leek together according to package directions for broccoli, omitting salt. Drain; reserve ¼ cup liquid. Add additional water, if needed, to make ¼ cup.

2. Combine milk, cornstarch, oregano and pepper sauce in medium saucepan. Stir in reserved ¼ cup liquid. Cook and stir over medium heat until mixture boils and thickens. Stir in cream cheese. Cook and stir until cheese melts. Stir in vegetables; heat through.

3. Serve vegetable mixture over pasta. Sprinkle with Romano cheese and parsley. Garnish as desired.

Makes 4 servings

saucy broccoli and spaghetti

jerk chicken and pasta

Jerk Sauce (recipe follows)

12 ounces boneless skinless chicken breasts

Nonstick cooking spray

1 cup canned fat-free reduced-sodium chicken broth

1 green bell pepper, sliced

2 green onions with tops, sliced

8 ounces uncooked fettuccine, cooked and kept warm

Grated Parmesan cheese (optional)

1. Prepare Jerk Sauce. Spread on both sides of chicken. Place in glass dish; refrigerate, covered, 15 to 30 minutes.

2. Spray medium skillet with cooking spray. Heat over medium heat until hot. Add chicken; cook 5 to 10 minutes or until browned and no longer pink in center. Add chicken broth, bell pepper and onions; bring to a boil. Reduce heat and simmer, uncovered, 5 to 7 minutes or until vegetables are crisp-tender and broth is reduced to thin sauce consistency.

3. Remove chicken from skillet and cut into slices. Toss fettuccine, chicken and vegetable mixture in large serving bowl. Sprinkle with Parmesan cheese, if desired.

Makes 4 servings

jerk sauce

¼ cup loosely packed fresh cilantro

2 tablespoons coarsely chopped fresh ginger

2 tablespoons black pepper

2 tablespoons lime juice

3 cloves garlic

1 tablespoon ground allspice

½ teaspoon curry powder

¼ teaspoon ground cloves

⅛ teaspoon ground red pepper

Combine all ingredients in food processor or blender; process until thick paste consistency.

Makes about ¼ cup

jerk chicken and pasta

caribbean shrimp with rice

1 package (12 ounces) frozen shrimp, thawed

½ cup fat-free reduced-sodium chicken broth

1 clove garlic, minced

1 teaspoon chili powder

½ teaspoon salt

½ teaspoon dried oregano leaves

1 cup frozen peas, thawed

½ cup diced tomatoes

2 cups cooked long-grain white rice

helpful hint

To make clean-up easier, spray the inside of the slow cooker with nonstick cooking spray before adding the food.

Slow Cooker Directions

Combine shrimp, broth, garlic, chili powder, salt and oregano in slow cooker. Cover and cook on LOW 2 hours. Add peas and tomatoes. Cover and cook on LOW 5 minutes. Stir in rice. Cover and cook on LOW an additional 5 minutes. *Makes 4 servings*

caribbean shrimp with rice

oriental pork stir-fry

1½ pounds pork
    tenderloin

2 teaspoons vegetable
    oil

1 teaspoon grated fresh
    ginger

1 clove garlic, minced

2 medium green bell
    peppers, cut into
    thin strips

1 (8-ounce) can sliced
    water chestnuts,
    drained

3 tablespoons soy sauce

1 tablespoon cornstarch

1½ cups cherry tomato
    halves

Partially freeze pork; cut pork into 3×½×⅛-inch strips. Preheat nonstick skillet over high heat; add oil. Stir-fry ginger and garlic in hot oil 30 seconds; remove from skillet. Add half of pork to skillet; stir-fry 5 minutes or until browned. Remove from skillet. Stir-fry remaining pork 5 minutes or until browned; remove from skillet. Add peppers and water chestnuts; stir-fry 3 to 4 minutes. Combine soy sauce and cornstarch; stir into vegetable mixture. Stir in pork; heat through. Add tomato halves, stirring to combine. Serve immediately.

Makes 6 servings

Prep Time: 20 minutes

*Favorite recipe from **National Pork Board***

helpful hint

When buying fresh ginger, select roots with smooth, unwrinkled skin. To use, peel the tough skin away to expose the tender root underneath; peel only as needed.

lighter stuffed peppers

1 can (10¾ ounces) reduced-fat condensed tomato soup, undiluted, divided

¼ cup water

8 ounces 93% lean ground turkey

1 cup cooked rice

¾ cup frozen corn, thawed

¼ cup sliced celery

¼ cup chopped red bell pepper

1 teaspoon dried Italian seasoning

½ teaspoon hot pepper sauce

2 green, yellow or red bell peppers, cut in half lengthwise and seeds removed

1. Blend ¼ cup soup and water in small bowl. Pour into 8×8-inch baking dish; set aside. Brown turkey in large nonstick skillet over medium-high heat; drain well. Combine remaining soup with cooked turkey, rice, corn, celery, chopped bell pepper, Italian seasoning and hot pepper sauce in large bowl; mix well.

2. Fill pepper halves equally with turkey mixture. Place stuffed peppers on top of soup mixture in baking dish. Cover and bake at 350°F 35 to 40 minutes. To serve, place peppers on serving dish and spoon remaining sauce from baking dish over peppers.

Makes 4 servings

lighter stuffed peppers

turkey vegetable crescent pie

2 cans (about 14 ounces) fat-free reduced-sodium chicken broth

1 medium onion, diced

1¼ pounds turkey tenderloins, cut into ¾-inch pieces

3 cups diced red potatoes

1 teaspoon chopped fresh rosemary *or* ½ teaspoon dried rosemary

¼ teaspoon salt

⅛ teaspoon black pepper

1 bag (16 ounces) frozen mixed vegetables

1 bag (10 ounces) frozen mixed vegetables

⅓ cup fat-free (skim) milk plus additional if necessary

3 tablespoons cornstarch

1 package (8 ounces) refrigerated reduced-fat crescent rolls

1. Bring broth to a boil in large saucepan. Add onion; reduce heat and simmer 3 minutes. Add turkey; return to a boil. Reduce heat, cover and simmer 7 to 9 minutes or until turkey is no longer pink. With slotted spoon, remove turkey from saucepan; place in 13×9-inch baking dish.

2. Return broth to a boil. Add potatoes, rosemary, salt and pepper; simmer 2 minutes. Return to a boil and stir in mixed vegetables. Simmer, covered, 7 to 8 minutes or until potatoes are tender. Remove vegetables with slotted spoon. Drain in colander set over bowl; reserve broth. Transfer vegetables to baking dish with turkey.

3. Preheat oven to 375°F. Blend ⅓ cup milk with cornstarch in small bowl until smooth. Add enough milk to reserved broth to equal 3 cups. Heat in large saucepan over medium-high heat; whisk in cornstarch mixture, stirring constantly until mixture comes to a boil. Boil 1 minute; remove from heat. Pour over turkey-vegetable mixture in baking dish.

4. Roll out crescent roll dough and separate at perforations; arrange dough pieces decoratively over top of turkey-vegetable mixture. Bake 13 to 15 minutes or until crust is golden brown. *Makes 8 servings*

turkey vegetable crescent pie

spicy pork chop casserole

Nonstick cooking spray

2 cups frozen corn

2 cups frozen diced hash brown potatoes

1 can (14½-ounces) diced tomatoes with basil, garlic and oregano, drained

2 teaspoons chili powder

1 teaspoon dried oregano leaves

½ teaspoon ground cumin

⅛ teaspoon crushed red pepper

1 teaspoon olive oil

4 boneless pork loin chops, cut about ¾ inch thick (12 ounces)

¼ teaspoon black pepper

¼ cup (1 ounce) shredded reduced-fat Monterey Jack cheese (optional)

1. Preheat oven to 375°F.

2. Lightly spray nonstick skillet with cooking spray. Add corn; cook and stir over medium-high heat about 5 minutes or until corn begins to brown. Add potatoes; cook and stir about 5 minutes more or until potatoes begin to brown. Add tomatoes, chili powder, oregano, cumin and red pepper; stir to combine.

3. Lightly spray 8×8×2-inch baking dish with cooking spray. Transfer corn mixture to prepared dish.

4. Wipe skillet with clean paper towel. Add oil and pork chops to skillet. Cook pork chops over medium-high heat until brown on one side. Remove pork chops; place, browned side up, on top of corn mixture in baking dish. Sprinkle with black pepper. Bake, uncovered, 20 minutes or until meat is juicy and barely pink in center. Sprinkle with cheese, if desired. Let stand 2 to 3 minutes. *Makes 4 servings*

Prep Time: 15 minutes
Bake Time: 20 minutes

spicy pork chop casserole

turkey and roasted pepper quesadillas

Nonstick cooking spray

8 (6-inch) corn tortillas

1 jar (7¼ ounces) roasted red peppers, drained and diced

4 ounces diced cooked turkey breast

1 cup (4 ounces) shredded part-skim mozzarella cheese

½ cup chopped fresh cilantro

½ cup salsa (optional)

helpful hint

To make a quick salsa, combine 1 cup chopped fresh tomato, 2 tablespoons minced onion, 2 tablespoons minced fresh cilantro, 2 tablespoons lime juice, ½ jalapeño pepper, seeded and minced, and 3 cloves garlic, minced, in a small bowl. Refrigerate until ready to serve.

1. Spray small nonstick skillet with cooking spray; heat over medium heat until hot. Brush 1 tortilla lightly on both sides with water. Heat in skillet 1 minute on each side or until hot.

2. Layer ¼ of the diced peppers, turkey, cheese and cilantro on tortilla. Top with second tortilla; press lightly. Brush top of tortilla with water. Flip quesadilla to heat second side. Cook 3 minutes or until ingredients are heated through. Remove from heat. Repeat with remaining tortillas.

3. Cut quesadillas into halves. Serve with salsa, if desired. *Makes 4 servings*

turkey and roasted pepper quesadillas

stir-fry vegetable pizza

**Nonstick cooking
spray**

**1 pound (about 5 cups)
fresh cut stir-fry
vegetables such as
broccoli, zucchini,
bell peppers and red
onions**

**1 (12-inch) prepared
bread-style pizza
crust**

⅓ cup pizza sauce

**¼ teaspoon red pepper
flakes (optional)**

**1½ cups (6 ounces)
shredded part-skim
mozzarella cheese**

1. Heat oven to 425°F.

2. Heat large nonstick skillet over medium-high heat
1 minute; coat with cooking spray. Add vegetables; stir-
fry 4 to 5 minutes or until crisp-tender.

3. Place pizza crust on large baking sheet; top with
pizza sauce. Sprinkle pepper flakes over sauce, if
desired. Arrange vegetables over sauce; top with cheese.

4. Bake 12 to 14 minutes or until crust is golden brown
and cheese is melted. Cut into 8 wedges.

Makes 4 servings

helpful hint

*Buy pre-cut vegetables from the salad bar to make
preparation for this recipe extra quick.*

oven-fried chicken

2 boneless skinless chicken breasts (about 4 ounces each), cut into halves

4 small skinless chicken drumsticks (about 2½ ounces each)

3 tablespoons all-purpose flour

½ teaspoon poultry seasoning

¼ teaspoon garlic salt

¼ teaspoon black pepper

1½ cups cornflakes, crushed

1 tablespoon dried parsley flakes

1 egg white

1 tablespoon water

Nonstick cooking spray

1. Preheat oven to 375°F. Rinse chicken. Pat dry with paper towels. Trim off any fat.

2. Combine flour, poultry seasoning, garlic salt and pepper in resealable plastic food storage bag. Combine cornflake crumbs and parsley in shallow bowl. Whisk together egg white and water in small bowl.

3. Add chicken to flour mixture, one or two pieces at a time. Seal bag; shake until chicken is well coated. Remove chicken from bag, shaking off excess flour. Dip into egg white mixture, coating all sides. Roll in crumb mixture. Place in shallow baking pan. Repeat with remaining chicken, flour mixture, egg white mixture and crumb mixture.

4. Lightly spray chicken pieces with cooking spray. Bake breast pieces 18 to 20 minutes or until no longer pink in center. Bake drumsticks about 25 minutes or until juices run clear. *Makes 4 servings*

oven-fried chicken

spinach-stuffed chicken breasts

4 boneless skinless chicken breasts (about 1 pound)

5 ounces frozen chopped spinach, thawed and squeezed dry

2 tablespoons freshly grated Parmesan cheese

1 teaspoon grated lemon peel

¼ teaspoon black pepper

Nonstick olive oil cooking spray

1 cup thinly sliced mushrooms

6 slices (2 ounces) thinly sliced low-fat turkey-ham

1 cup white grape juice

1. Trim fat from chicken; discard. Place each chicken breast between 2 sheets of plastic wrap. Pound with meat mallet until chicken is about ¼ inch thick.

2. Preheat oven to 350°F. Pat spinach dry with paper towels. Combine spinach, Parmesan, lemon peel and pepper in large bowl. Spray small nonstick skillet with cooking spray; add mushrooms. Cook and stir over medium heat 3 to 4 minutes or until tender.

3. Arrange 1½ slices turkey-ham over each chicken breast. Spread each with one-fourth of spinach mixture. Top each with mushrooms. Beginning with longer side, roll chicken tightly. Tie with kitchen string.

4. Place stuffed chicken breasts, seam side down, in 9-inch square baking pan. Lightly spray chicken with cooking spray. Pour white grape juice over top. Bake 30 minutes or until chicken is no longer pink.

5. Remove string; cut chicken rolls into ½-inch diagonal slices. Arrange on plate. Pour pan juices over chicken. Garnish as desired. *Makes 4 servings*

spinach-stuffed chicken breast

jalapeño-lime chicken

1 tablespoon olive oil

1 tablespoon lime juice

1 jalapeño pepper,*
   seeded and diced

1 teaspoon cumin

2 cloves garlic, minced

1 teaspoon lime zest

¼ teaspoon salt

1 pound boneless
   skinless chicken
   breast

Sliced jalapeño
   peppers* and black
   olives for garnish

*Jalapeño peppers can sting and
irritate the skin; wear rubber gloves
when handling peppers and do not
touch eyes. Wash hands after
handling.*

1. Combine oil, lime juice, jalapeño, cumin, garlic, lime zest and salt in small bowl. Brush mixture on both sides of chicken. Cover with plastic wrap and let marinate in refrigerator 30 minutes or up to 8 hours.

2. Preheat grill to medium-high. Grill chicken 5 to 6 minutes on each side or until no longer pink in center. Garnish with jalapeño and black olive slices.

Makes 4 servings

helpful hint

Cleanup is easier if the grill rack is coated with vegetable oil or nonstick cooking spray before grilling.

lemon salmon and spinach pasta

¾ **pound salmon fillet**

8 **ounces uncooked fettuccine**

1 **teaspoon finely grated lemon peel**

¼ **teaspoon crushed red pepper**

2 **cloves garlic, minced**

4 **teaspoons butter**

2 **tablespoons lemon juice**

3 **cups washed baby spinach leaves**

½ **cup shredded carrot**

1. Rinse salmon; pat dry with paper towels. Remove skin from salmon; discard. Cut fish into ½-inch pieces.

2. Cook fettuccine according to package directions, omitting salt. Drain. Return to hot pan; set aside.

3. Meanwhile, melt butter in large skillet over medium-high heat. Add salmon, lemon peel, red pepper and garlic; cook 4 to 7 minutes or until salmon flakes easily when tested with fork. Gently stir in lemon juice.

4. Add salmon mixture, spinach leaves and carrot to hot cooked linguine. Gently toss to combine. Serve immediately. *Makes 4 servings*

Prep Time: 15 minutes
Cook Time: 4 to 7 minutes

lemon salmon and spinach pasta

fettuccine gorgonzola with sun-dried tomatoes

4 ounces sun-dried tomatoes, not oil packed

8 ounces uncooked spinach or tri-color fettuccine

1 cup low-fat cottage cheese

½ cup plain nonfat yogurt

½ cup (2 ounces) crumbled Gorgonzola cheese

⅛ teaspoon white pepper

1. Place sun-dried tomatoes in small bowl; pour hot water over to cover. Let stand 15 minutes or until tomatoes are soft. Drain well; cut into strips. Cook pasta according to package directions, omitting salt. Drain well. Cover to keep warm.

2. Combine cottage cheese and yogurt in food processor or blender; process until smooth. Heat cottage cheese mixture in small saucepan over low heat. Add Gorgonzola and white pepper; stir until cheese is melted.

3. Return pasta to saucepan; add tomatoes. Pour cheese mixture over pasta; mix well. Garnish as desired. Serve immediately. *Makes 4 servings*

pasta with spinach and ricotta

8 ounces uncooked tri-colored rotini

1 box (10 ounces) frozen chopped spinach, thawed and squeezed dry

2 teaspoons bottled minced garlic

1 cup fat-free or part-skim ricotta cheese

3 tablespoons grated Parmesan cheese, divided

1. Cook pasta according to package directions; drain.

2. While pasta is cooking, coat skillet with nonstick cooking spray; heat over medium-low heat. Add spinach and garlic; cook and stir 5 minutes. Stir in ricotta cheese, half of Parmesan cheese and ½ cup water; season with salt and pepper to taste.

3. Add pasta to skillet; stir until well blended. Sprinkle with remaining Parmesan cheese. *Makes 4 servings*

Tip: For a special touch, garnish with fresh basil leaves.

Prep and Cook Time: 24 minutes

fettuccine gorgonzola with sun-dried tomatoes

spicy mesquite chicken fettuccine

8 ounces uncooked fettuccine

1 tablespoon chili powder

1 teaspoon ground cumin

1 teaspoon paprika

¼ teaspoon ground red pepper

2 teaspoons vegetable oil

1 pound mesquite marinated chicken breasts, cut into bite-size pieces

1. Cook pasta according to package directions, omitting salt. Drain; set aside.

2. Combine chili powder, cumin, paprika and ground red pepper in small bowl; set aside.

3. Heat oil in large nonstick skillet over medium-high heat until hot. Add chili powder mixture; cook 30 seconds, stirring constantly. Add chicken; cook and stir 5 to 6 minutes or until no longer pink in center and lightly browned. Add pasta to skillet; stir. Cook 1 to 2 minutes or until heated through. Sprinkle with additional chili powder, if desired. *Makes 4 servings*

lemon-capered pork tenderloin

1 boneless pork tenderloin (about 1½ pounds)

1 tablespoon crushed capers

1 teaspoon dried rosemary leaves

⅛ teaspoon black pepper

1 cup water

¼ cup lemon juice

1. Preheat oven to 350°F. Trim fat from tenderloin; discard. Set tenderloin aside.

2. Combine capers, rosemary and pepper in small bowl. Rub mixture over tenderloin. Place tenderloin in shallow roasting pan. Pour water and lemon juice over tenderloin.

3. Bake, uncovered, 1 hour or until thermometer inserted into thickest part of tenderloin registers 160°F. Remove from oven; cover with foil. Allow to stand 10 minutes. Cut evenly into 8 slices before serving. Garnish as desired. *Makes 8 servings*

spicy mesquite chicken fettuccine

black beans & rice-stuffed chilies

2 large poblano chili peppers*

½ (15½-ounce) can black beans, rinsed and drained

½ cup cooked brown rice

⅓ cup mild or medium chunky salsa

⅓ cup shredded reduced-fat Cheddar cheese or pepper Jack cheese, divided

*Poblano peppers can sting and irritate the skin; wear rubber gloves when handling peppers and do not touch eyes. Wash hands after handling peppers.

1. Preheat oven to 375°F. Lightly spray shallow baking pan with nonstick olive oil cooking spray.

2. Cut thin slice from one side of each pepper. Chop pepper slices; set aside. In medium saucepan, cook remaining peppers in boiling water 6 minutes. Drain and rinse with cold water. Remove and discard seeds and membranes.

3. Stir together beans, rice, salsa, chopped pepper and ¼ cup cheese. Spoon into peppers, mounding mixture. Place peppers in prepared pan. Cover with foil. Bake 12 to 15 minutes or until heated through.

4. Sprinkle with remaining cheese. Bake 2 minutes more or until cheese melts.   *Makes 2 servings*

helpful hint

Poblano peppers are very dark green, large triangular-shaped chilies with pointed ends. Poblanos are usually 3½ to 5 inches long.

black beans & rice-stuffed chili

chicken with white beans and spinach

¾ **pound boneless skinless chicken breasts, cut in ¾-inch pieces**

¼ **teaspoon salt**

¼ **teaspoon black pepper**

1 **tablespoon olive oil**

3 **cups thinly sliced onion**

4 **cloves garlic, minced**

2 **cans (19 ounces each) white beans, such as Great Northern or cannellini, rinsed and drained**

1 **small dried hot pepper, crumbled** *or* ¼ **teaspoon red pepper flakes**

¾ **cup water**

1 **package (10 ounces) fresh spinach, washed and torn**

1. Preheat oven to 425°F. Spray shallow 2-quart casserole dish with nonstick cooking spray; set aside.

2. Sprinkle chicken with salt and pepper. Heat olive oil in nonstick skillet over medium heat. Add chicken; cook without stirring 2 minutes or until golden. Turn chicken; cook 2 minutes. Add onion; cook and stir until onion is crisp-tender, about 5 minutes. Add garlic and cook 1 minute.

3. Stir in beans, hot pepper and ¾ cup water. Cook, stirring constantly, about 3 minutes. Transfer to prepared casserole dish. Cover; bake 10 minutes.

4. Meanwhile, drop spinach into pot of boiling water; cook 30 seconds or until spinach turns bright green. Remove from water with slotted spoon; drain.

5. Add spinach to bean mixture; stir gently. Cover; bake 15 minutes. *Makes 6 servings*

buttery pepper and citrus broiled fish

3 tablespoons MOLLY MCBUTTER® Flavored Sprinkles

1 tablespoon MRS. DASH® Lemon Pepper Blend

1 tablespoon lime juice

2 teaspoons honey

1 pound boneless white fish fillets

Combine first 4 ingredients in small bowl; mix well. Broil fish 6 to 8 inches from heat, turning once. Spread with Lemon Pepper mixture. Broil an additional 4 to 5 minutes. *Makes 4 servings*

Preparation Time: 5 minutes
Cooking Time: 10 minutes

chicken with rosemary-peach glaze

4 boneless skinless chicken breasts (about 1 pound)

2 tablespoons reduced-sodium soy sauce, divided

⅓ cup peach preserves

1 sprig fresh rosemary *or* 1 teaspoon dried rosemary leaves

1 tablespoon lemon juice

1 clove garlic, minced

2 cups cooked wild rice and long-grain rice mix

1. Preheat broiler. Spray baking sheet with nonstick cooking spray. Sprinkle chicken with 1 tablespoon soy sauce; place on prepared baking sheet. Broil 4 to 6 inches from heat 3 minutes; turn and broil 3 minutes longer.

2. Meanwhile, combine preserves, rosemary, lemon juice, remaining 1 tablespoon soy sauce and garlic in small saucepan. Cook over medium-low heat 5 minutes.

3. Brush sauce over chicken; broil 2 minutes. Turn and brush with sauce. Broil 2 minutes longer or until chicken is no longer pink in center. Discard any remaining sauce. Serve chicken with rice.

Makes 4 servings

Prep Time: 5 minutes
Cook Time: 15 minutes

199

spiced turkey with fruit salsa

6 ounces turkey breast tenderloin

2 teaspoons lime juice

1 teaspoon mesquite seasoning blend or ground cumin

½ cup frozen pitted sweet cherries, thawed and cut into halves*

¼ cup chunky salsa

Drained canned sweet cherries can be substituted for frozen cherries.

1. Prepare grill for direct grilling. Brush both sides of turkey with lime juice. Sprinkle with mesquite seasoning.

2. Grill turkey over medium coals 15 to 20 minutes or until turkey is no longer pink in center and juices run clear, turning once.

3. Meanwhile, stir together cherries and salsa.

4. Thinly slice turkey. Spoon salsa mixture over turkey.

Makes 2 servings

blackberry-glazed pork medallions

⅓ cup no-sugar-added seedless blackberry spread

1½ tablespoons red wine vinegar

1 tablespoon sugar

¼ teaspoon red pepper flakes

1 teaspoon vegetable oil

1 pound pork tenderloin, cut in ¼-inch slices

¼ teaspoon dried thyme leaves, divided

¼ teaspoon salt, divided

1. Whisk blackberry spread, vinegar, sugar and red pepper flakes in small bowl until blended; set aside.

2. Heat large nonstick skillet over medium-high heat until hot. Coat skillet with oil; tilt to coat bottom. Add half of pork slices; sprinkle with half of thyme and half of salt. Cook 2 minutes; turn and cook 1 minute on other side. Remove pork from skillet and set aside. Repeat with remaining pork, thyme and salt.

3. Add blackberry mixture to skillet; bring to a boil over high heat. Add reserved pork slices, discarding any accumulated juices. Cook about 4 minutes, turning constantly, until pork is richly glazed.

Makes 4 servings

spiced turkey with fruit salsa

spicy caribbean pork medallions

6 ounces pork
tenderloin

1 teaspoon Caribbean
jerk seasoning

Nonstick olive oil
cooking spray

⅓ cup pineapple juice

1 teaspoon brown
mustard

½ teaspoon cornstarch

1. Cut tenderloin into ½-inch-thick slices. Place each slice between 2 pieces of plastic wrap. Pound to ¼-inch thickness. Rub both sides of pork pieces with jerk seasoning.

2. Lightly spray large nonstick skillet with cooking spray; heat over medium heat until hot. Add pork. Cook 2 to 3 minutes or until no longer pink, turning once. Remove from skillet. Keep warm.

3. Stir together pineapple juice, mustard and cornstarch until smooth. Add to skillet. Cook and stir over medium heat until mixture comes to a boil and thickens slightly. Spoon over pork. *Makes 2 servings*

chicken pomodoro with tomato basil garlic

4 teaspoons olive oil

8 boneless skinless
chicken breast
halves

8 ounces fresh
mushrooms, sliced

2 cans (14¼ ounces)
Italian-style stewed
tomatoes

8 teaspoons MRS.
DASH® Tomato
Basil Garlic

½ cup semi-dry white
wine (optional)

Heat oil in nonstick skillet. Add chicken and brown over medium heat, about 10 minutes, turning once. Add remaining ingredients. Bring to a boil; reduce heat and simmer, uncovered, 15 minutes. *Makes 8 servings*

Preparation Time: 10 minutes
Cooking Time: 25 minutes

spicy caribbean pork medallions

lemon-asparagus chicken with dill

½ **cup uncooked rice**

1 **teaspoon chicken bouillon granules**

1 **cup water, divided**

1 **cup asparagus, cut into 2-inch pieces**

Nonstick cooking spray

6 **ounces boneless skinless chicken breasts, cut into bite-size pieces**

1 **tablespoon lemon juice**

2 **teaspoons olive oil**

1½ **teaspoons dried dill weed**

⅛ **teaspoon salt**

2 **tablespoons finely chopped parsley**

1. Prepare rice according to package directions, adding bouillon granules to ½ cup water.

2. Meanwhile, place remaining ½ cup water in 12-inch nonstick skillet; bring to a boil. Add asparagus; return to a boil; reduce heat and simmer, covered, 3 minutes or until crisp-tender. Drain; set aside. Wipe out skillet with paper towel.

3. Coat same skillet with cooking spray. Heat over medium-high heat until hot. Add chicken; cook and stir 3 minutes or until no longer pink. Remove from heat; add asparagus. Cover and keep warm.

4. Combine lemon juice, oil, dill and salt in small bowl.

5. Add rice, lemon juice mixture and parsley to chicken mixture; stir until blended.

Makes 2 (1½-cup) servings

Lemon Chicken with Peas & Dill: Substitute ½ cup thawed frozen peas, for asparagus; omitting water. Add peas to chicken in step 3 after chicken is cooked.

lemon-asparagus chicken with dill

BREAD BAKING FUNDAMENTALS

Baking bread from scratch may seem like a big task to take on yourself. However, there are many kinds of breads, such as muffins and scones, that can be made with little time or effort. Freshly baked yeast breads can easily be made in a bread machine. Bread is a great accompaniment to any meal, good for sandwiches, perfect for breakfast and even snacking.

Types of Bread

Breads fall into one of two main categories depending on the leavening agent. (Leavening gives bread its height and texture.) Yeast-leavened bread makes up much of the bread available in bakeries and supermarkets. It can also be made at home. Although it requires some time to make, hot bread from the oven is a wonderful reward for your efforts. Since you are just starting out in the kitchen, quick breads may be the route for you. As their name suggests, they are quick and easy to make.

For quick batter breads, such as muffins, coffee cakes and tea breads, add the combined liquid ingredients to the combined dry ingredients and stir with a wooden spoon or rubber spatula just until the mixture is evenly moistened. The batter should look lumpy when it goes into the prepared pan(s). Too much stirring or beating will give the breads a tough texture with lots of holes and tunnels. Muffins and tea breads are completely baked when a wooden toothpick inserted into the center comes out clean.

For quick dough breads, such as biscuits and scones, cut the solid fat into the dry ingredients until the mixture resembles coarse crumbs. Add the combined liquid ingredients and stir the mixture just until the dough clings together. These doughs may be kneaded very briefly to bring the dough together so that it can be shaped. Too much kneading will make the breads mealy and tough. Biscuits and scones are done when their top and bottom crusts are an even golden brown color.

Storing Bread

Once the bread has cooled completely (about 3 hours), wrap it in plastic wrap or place it in an airtight plastic food storage bag. Store the bread at room temperature for up to 4 days; placing it in the refrigerator actually causes it to become stale faster. Most breads, especially fruit, such as banana bread may only keep for 2 or 3 days at room temperature. If it is well wrapped, bread can be frozen for up to six months.

Bread Machine Basics

Bread machines have revolutionized the world of bread baking. It no longer requires a lot of time and effort to make delicious homemade bread—it's now as easy as pressing a button. Even shaped breads and pizza doughs can be made quickly with the magic of this wonderful appliance. What could be better than a fresh, warm loaf of bread to enjoy with a family dinner, a leisurely weekend brunch, a festive holiday meal, or even for no occasion whatsoever. If you can measure ingredients, you can bake bread—it's as simple as that! Before starting, be sure to read the manufacturer's instructions, because all bread machines are slightly different. But no matter what bread machine you use, there are a few basics to keep in mind.

What Size Is Your Bread Machine?

You should know the size of your bread machine before making a loaf of bread. If you are unsure, check the manual or determine the size by measuring how much water the bread pan can hold.
- A 1½-pound machine pan can hold about 12 cups of water.
- A 2-pound bread machine pan can hold about 13 to 15 cups of water.

You can always make a loaf of bread that is smaller than the bread machine's capacity, but you can never make a loaf that is larger than its machine's capacity. Once you know the size of your bread machine, you also need to know what size loaf the recipe makes. If it is not stated in the recipe, use this rule of thumb. a 1½-pound loaf calls for about 3 cups of flour while a 2-pound loaf calls for about 4 cups of flour.

Adding Ingredients

•Follow the manufacturer's instructions for the proper order to add ingredients. Some bread machines require dry ingredients to be added first while others require liquids to be added first. If you don't follow your manufacturer's recommendations, your bread may be unsatisfactory.

•To be sure that you don't omit any ingredients, assemble all your ingredients on the counter in the order recommended by the owner's manual.

•Except for dairy products like milk and eggs, ingredients should be added at room temperature.

BASIC BREAD BAKING

hawaiian fruit and nut quick bread

2 cups all-purpose flour

1 tablespoon orange-
    flavored instant
    drink powder

2 teaspoons baking soda

1 teaspoon cinnamon

¾ cup granulated sugar

¾ cup light brown sugar

¾ cup chopped
    macadamia nuts

½ cup shredded coconut

¾ cup canola oil

2 eggs

2 teaspoons rum extract

2 cups chopped fresh
    mango

1. Preheat oven to 350°F. Lightly grease 9×3-inch loaf pan. Set aside.

2. Sift flour, drink powder, baking soda and cinnamon into medium bowl. Stir in sugars, macadamia nuts and coconut. Combine oil, eggs and rum extract in separate medium bowl. Add to dry mixture; stir to mix well. Stir in mango.

3. Spoon batter into prepared pan. Bake 60 to 70 minutes or until bread is light golden brown in color and pulls away from sides of pan. Cool in pan 10 minutes. Remove to wire rack and cool completely.

Makes 1 loaf

hawaiian fruit and nut quick bread

easy raspberry-peach danish

1 loaf (16 ounces) frozen white bread dough, thawed

⅓ cup no-added-sugar raspberry spread

1 can (15 ounces) sliced peaches in extra light syrup, drained and chopped

Egg white (optional)

½ cup powdered sugar

2 to 3 teaspoons orange juice

¼ cup chopped pecans, toasted

1. Preheat oven to 350°F. Spray 2 baking sheets with nonstick cooking spray.

2. Place dough on lightly floured surface. Cut dough in half. Roll each half into 12×7-inch rectangle. Place 1 rectangle on each prepared baking sheet.

3. Spread half of raspberry spread over center third of each dough rectangle. Sprinkle peaches over raspberry spread.

4. On both long sides of each dough rectangle, make 2-inch long cuts from edges towards filling at 1-inch intervals. Starting at one end, alternately fold opposite strips of dough over filling.

5. Cover; let rise in warm place about 1 hour or until nearly doubled in size. Bake 15 to 20 minutes or until golden. If deeper golden color is desired, lightly brush egg white over tops of loaves during last 5 minutes of baking. Remove baked loaves from baking sheet. Cool slightly.

6. Combine powdered sugar and enough orange juice in small bowl until drizzling consistency is reached. Drizzle over both loaves. Sprinkle pecans over top.

Makes 32 servings (2 loaves)

Prep Time: 15 minutes
Rising Time: 1 hour
Bake Time: 15 to 20 minutes

easy raspberry-peach danish

apple cheddar scones

1½ cups all-purpose flour

½ cup toasted wheat germ

3 tablespoons sugar

2 teaspoons baking powder

½ teaspoon salt

2 tablespoons butter

1 small Washington Rome apple, cored and chopped

¼ cup shredded Cheddar cheese

1 large egg white

½ cup low-fat (1%) milk

helpful hint

Wheat germ, the embryo of the wheat berry, has a nutty flavor and is very oily. It is sold in both its toasted and natural forms.

1. Heat oven to 400°F. Grease an 8-inch round cake pan. In medium-size bowl, combine flour, wheat germ, sugar, baking powder and salt. With two knives or pastry blender, cut in butter until the size of coarse crumbs. Toss chopped apple and cheese in flour mixture.

2. Beat together egg white and milk until well combined. Add to flour mixture, mixing with fork until dough forms. Turn dough out onto lightly floured surface and knead 6 times.

3. Spread dough evenly in cake pan and score deeply with knife into 6 wedges. Bake 25 to 30 minutes or until top springs back when gently pressed. Let stand 5 minutes; remove from pan. Cool before serving.

Makes 6 scones

*Favorite recipe from **Washington Apple Commission***

one-bowl focaccia

1¼ cups warm water
(110°F)

1 package
(1½ teaspoons)
active dry yeast

¼ cup plus 2 tablespoons
extra virgin olive oil

3 cups unbleached all-
purpose flour

1½ teaspoons salt

Additional flour for
kneading

Toppings of your
choice*

Suggested toppings: ½ teaspoon black pepper and ½ teaspoon red pepper flakes; 1 tablespoon Italian seasoning; 1 tablespoon dried minced onion and 1 tablespoon dried basil; 1½ tablespoons chopped mixed fresh herbs (basil, rosemary, sage and parsley); 1 can (8 ounces) prepared pizza sauce

1. Combine water and yeast in large bowl. Stir to dissolve yeast. Stir in ¼ cup olive oil.

2. Mix flour and salt in separate bowl. Add to yeast mixture. Stir with large spoon until dough forms and pulls away from side of bowl.

3. Dip hands lightly in flour and knead dough in bowl, flouring hands as needed, until dough is smooth and springy, 3 to 5 minutes. Lift dough from bowl and spray bowl lightly with nonstick olive oil cooking spray. Return dough to bowl, then turn so oiled side is up.

4. Cover with plastic wrap and let rise in warm (85°F) place about 1 hour or until doubled in bulk.

5. Oil 15½×10½ inch baking pan with 1 tablespoon olive oil. Uncover dough and, without kneading or punching down, place into prepared pan. Spread and stretch dough over bottom of pan with hands.

6. Cover crust with waxed paper that has been sprayed with cooking spray. Let rise in warm place 45 minutes to 1 hour or until doubled in bulk.

7. Preheat oven to 400°F. Uncover dough, spread with remaining 1 tablespoon olive oil and sprinkle with your choice of toppings. Make indentations in dough with fingertips. Bake about 25 minutes or until edges are golden brown. Cut into 12 wedges. Serve warm or at room temperature. *Makes 12 servings*

lots o' chocolate bread

⅔ cup packed light
    brown sugar

½ cup butter, softened

2 cups miniature
    semisweet chocolate
    chips, divided

2 eggs

2½ cups all-purpose flour

1½ cups applesauce

1½ teaspoons vanilla

1 teaspoon baking soda

1 teaspoon baking
    powder

½ teaspoon salt

1 tablespoon shortening
    (do not use butter,
    margarine, spread
    or oil)

Preheat oven to 350°F. Grease 5 (5½×3-inch) mini loaf pans. Beat brown sugar and butter in large bowl with electric mixer until creamy. Melt 1 cup miniature chocolate chips; cool slightly and add to sugar mixture with eggs. Add flour, applesauce, vanilla, baking soda, baking powder and salt; beat until well mixed. Stir in ½ cup chocolate chips. Spoon batter into prepared pans; bake 35 to 40 minutes or until centers crack and are dry to the touch. Cool 10 minutes before removing from pans.

Place remaining ½ cup chocolate chips and shortening in small microwavable bowl. Microwave at HIGH 1 minute; stir. If necessary, microwave at HIGH an additional 15 seconds at a time, stirring after each heating. Drizzle warm loaves with glaze. Cool completely. *Makes 5 mini loaves*

lots o' chocolate bread

strawberry muffins

CRISCO® No-Stick
Cooking Spray

1½ cups all-purpose flour

1½ teaspoons baking
powder

¼ teaspoon salt

⅓ cup granulated sugar

1 egg

½ cup buttermilk

⅓ cup CRISCO® Oil

¼ cup SMUCKER'S®
Strawberry Jam

¾ cup fresh
strawberries, diced

Heat oven to 375°F. Spray muffin tins with CRISCO®
No-Stick Cooking Spray.

Combine flour, baking powder, salt and sugar. Beat egg
with buttermilk. Stir in CRISCO® Oil and strawberry
jam.

Stir liquid and strawberries into dry ingredients until
just blended. Divide mixture between prepared muffin
tins.

Bake at 375°F. for 15 to 18 minutes, or until toothpick
inserted in center comes out clean.

Cool in tins 5 minutes. Serve warm

Makes 12 muffins

The muffins are best if baked just before serving. If
made in advance, reheat at 300°F wrapped in foil for
10 minutes.

popovers

1 cup all-purpose flour

1 cup milk

3 large eggs

1 tablespoon butter, at
room temperature

½ teaspoon salt

1. Heat oven to 375°F. Grease and flour 12 muffin cups
or six 6-ounce custard cups.

2. Fit processor with steel blade. Add all ingredients to
the work bowl. Process 2½ minutes continuously.

3. Pour batter into prepared cups, filling each about
¾ full. Bake 45 to 50 minutes or until dark brown and
crispy. Serve immediately.

Makes 6 large or 12 small popovers

strawberry muffins

CRISCO® No-Stick
Cooking Spray

1½ cups all-purpose flour

1½ teaspoons baking
powder

¼ teaspoon salt

⅓ cup granulated sugar

1 egg

½ cup buttermilk

⅓ cup CRISCO® Oil

¼ cup SMUCKER'S®
Strawberry Jam

¾ cup fresh
strawberries, diced

Heat oven to 375°F. Spray muffin tins with CRISCO®
No-Stick Cooking Spray.

Combine flour, baking powder, salt and sugar. Beat egg
with buttermilk. Stir in CRISCO® Oil and strawberry
jam.

Stir liquid and strawberries into dry ingredients until
just blended. Divide mixture between prepared muffin
tins.

Bake at 375°F. for 15 to 18 minutes, or until toothpick
inserted in center comes out clean.

Cool in tins 5 minutes. Serve warm

Makes 12 muffins

The muffins are best if baked just before serving. If
made in advance, reheat at 300°F wrapped in foil for
10 minutes.

popovers

1 cup all-purpose flour

1 cup milk

3 large eggs

1 tablespoon butter, at
room temperature

½ teaspoon salt

1. Heat oven to 375°F. Grease and flour 12 muffin cups
or six 6-ounce custard cups.

2. Fit processor with steel blade. Add all ingredients to
the work bowl. Process 2½ minutes continuously.

3. Pour batter into prepared cups, filling each about
¾ full. Bake 45 to 50 minutes or until dark brown and
crispy. Serve immediately.

Makes 6 large or 12 small popovers

dinner rolls

1½ Pounds Dough
 ¾ cup milk
 1 egg
 ⅓ cup shortening
 1 teaspoon salt
 3 cups all-purpose flour
 3 tablespoons sugar
 1½ teaspoons active dry yeast

2 Pounds Dough
 1 cup milk
 2 eggs
 ½ cup shortening
 1½ teaspoons salt
 4 cups all-purpose flour
 ¼ cup sugar
 2 teaspoons active dry yeast

1. Measuring carefully, place all ingredients in bread machine pan in order specified by owner's manual. Program dough cycle setting; press start. For 1½ pounds dough, grease 13×9-inch baking pan; set aside. For 2 pounds dough, grease 2 (8-inch) square baking pans; set aside.

2. When cycle is complete, remove dough to lightly floured surface. If necessary, knead in additional all-purpose flour to make dough easy to handle. For 1½ pounds dough, divide into 18 equal pieces; for 2 pounds dough, divide into 24 equal pieces. Shape each dough piece into smooth ball. Place in prepared pan(s). Cover with clean towel; let rise in warm, draft-free place 45 minutes or until doubled in size.

3. Preheat oven to 375°F. Bake 15 to 20 minutes or until golden brown. Remove from pan(s); cool on wire rack(s). *Makes 18 to 24 rolls*

morning muffins with blueberries

½ cup plus 1 tablespoon
   sugar, divided

⅛ teaspoon ground
   cinnamon

1¾ cups all-purpose flour

2 teaspoons baking
   powder

½ teaspoon salt

½ cup milk

¼ cup vegetable oil

1 egg

1 teaspoon vanilla

1 teaspoon grated `
   orange peel

1 cup fresh or frozen
   blueberries, thawed
   and dried

1. Preheat oven to 400°F. Grease or paper-line 12 regular-size (2½-inch) muffin cups. Combine 1 tablespoon sugar and cinnamon in small bowl; set aside.

2. Combine flour, remaining ½ cup sugar, baking powder and salt in large bowl. Combine milk, oil, egg, vanilla and orange peel in small bowl. Mix until blended. Make a well in flour mixture; add milk mixture; stir just until moistened. Fold in blueberries. Spoon evenly into prepared muffin cups, filling about ⅔ full.

3. Bake 15 to 18 minutes or until toothpick inserted into centers comes out clean. Remove muffins from oven. Immediately sprinkle sugar mixture over hot muffins. Transfer to wire racks. Serve warm.

Makes 12 muffins

helpful hint

Remove muffins from their cups immediately after baking and cool them on a wire rack. They are best when served warm. Stored in an airtight plastic bag, muffins will stay fresh for several days. For longer storage, wrap and freeze. To reheat, wrap frozen muffins in foil and heat in a 350°F oven for 15 to 20 minutes. For best flavor, use frozen muffins within one month.

pesto roll-ups

1¼ cups water

2 tablespoons butter, softened

1 teaspoon salt

2¾ cups all-purpose flour

1 teaspoon sugar

1 teaspoon dried basil leaves

1½ teaspoons active dry yeast

1 cup prepared pesto

1. Measuring carefully, place all ingredients except pesto in bread machine pan in order specified by owner's manual. Program dough cycle setting; press start. (Do not use delay cycle.) Lightly grease 9-inch square baking pan; set aside.

2. When cycle is complete, remove dough to lightly floured surface. If necessary, knead in additional all-purpose flour to make dough easy to handle. Roll dough into 12-inch square; spread with pesto. Roll up tightly in jelly-roll fashion; pinch edge to seal. With sharp knife, evenly slice loaf into 9 pieces.

3. Place slices, cut sides up, in prepared pan. Cover with clean towel; let rise in warm, draft-free place 45 minutes or until doubled in size.

4. Preheat oven to 350°F. Bake rolls 35 to 40 minutes or until golden brown. Let cool slightly on wire rack. Serve warm.

Makes 9 rolls

cinnamon-date scones

4 tablespoons sugar, divided

¼ teaspoon ground cinnamon

2 cups all-purpose flour

2½ teaspoons baking powder

½ teaspoon salt

5 tablespoons cold butter

½ cup chopped pitted dates

2 eggs

⅓ cup half-and-half or milk

Preheat oven to 425°F. Combine 2 tablespoons sugar and cinnamon in small bowl; set aside. Combine flour, remaining 2 tablespoons sugar, baking powder and salt in medium bowl. Cut in butter with pastry blender or 2 knives until mixture resembles coarse crumbs. Stir in dates.

Beat eggs in another small bowl with fork. Add half-and-half; beat until well blended. Reserve 1 tablespoon egg mixture. Stir remaining egg mixture into flour mixture. Stir until soft dough clings together and forms ball.

Turn out dough onto well-floured surface. Knead dough gently 10 to 12 times. Roll dough into 9×6-inch rectangle. Cut rectangle into 6 (3-inch) squares. Cut each square diagonally in half. Place triangles 2 inches apart on ungreased baking sheets. Brush with reserved egg mixture; sprinkle with reserved cinnamon-sugar mixture. Bake 10 to 12 minutes or until golden brown. Immediately remove from baking sheets; cool on wire racks 10 minutes. Serve warm. *Makes 12 scones*

cinnamon-date scones

berry bran muffins

2 cups bran cereal

1¼ cups fat-free (skim) milk

½ cup packed brown sugar

1 egg, lightly beaten

¼ cup vegetable oil

1 teaspoon vanilla

1¼ cups all-purpose flour

1 tablespoon baking powder

¼ teaspoon salt

1 cup blueberries, fresh or frozen (partially thawed if frozen)

Preheat oven to 350°F. Line muffin pan with paper baking cups.

Mix cereal and milk in medium bowl. Let stand 5 minutes to soften. Add brown sugar, egg, oil and vanilla. Beat well. Combine flour, baking powder and salt in large bowl. Stir in cereal mixture until dry ingredients are just moistened. Gently fold in berries.

Fill muffin cups almost to top. Bake 20 to 25 minutes or until toothpick inserted into centers comes out clean. Serve warm.   *Makes 12 servings*

quick garlic-onion ring

¼ cup finely chopped green onions

1 tablespoon butter or margarine, melted

2 cloves garlic, minced

1 package (10 biscuit size) regular or buttermilk flaky biscuits

Preheat oven to 400°F. Combine onions, butter and garlic in small bowl; set aside.

Separate dough into individual biscuits. Gently pull apart each biscuit to separate into two halves, making 20 pieces.

Brush one side of each piece with garlic-onion mixture. Arrange pieces, onion-side up and overlapping, in 9-inch circle on ungreased baking sheet.

Bake 10 to 12 minutes until golden brown.
Makes 1 ring or 10 servings

berry bran muffins

peanut butter chip nutbread

½ cup shortening

¾ cup sugar

2 eggs

1¾ cups all-purpose flour

1 teaspoon baking soda

1 teaspoon salt

½ teaspoon ground cinnamon

¼ teaspoon ground nutmeg

1¼ cups applesauce

1⅔ cups (10-ounce package) REESE'S® Peanut Butter Chips

½ cup chopped pecans

½ cup golden raisins

1. Heat oven to 350°F. Grease and flour 9×5×3-inch loaf pan.

2. Beat shortening, sugar and eggs in large bowl until fluffy. Stir together flour, baking soda, salt, cinnamon and nutmeg; add alternately with applesauce to sugar mixture, mixing well after each addition. Stir in peanut butter chips, pecans and raisins.

3. Bake 1 hour 15 minutes or until wooden pick inserted in center comes out clean. Cool 10 minutes; remove from pan to wire rack. Cool completely.

Makes 1 loaf (14 servings)

herbed cheese biscuits

2 cups sifted all-purpose flour

3 teaspoons double-acting baking powder

2 teaspoons dill

1 teaspoon salt

⅓ CRISCO® Stick or ⅓ cup CRISCO® Shortening

½ cup shredded sharp Cheddar or Swiss cheese

¾ cup milk

Preheat oven to 425°F.

In a bowl, mix flour, baking powder, dill and salt. With a pastry blender, 2 knives or a fork, cut in CRISCO® Shortening until mixture looks like coarse meal. Stir in shredded cheese. Add milk and stir just until dough holds together.

Place on a lightly floured surface and knead lightly; roll ¾ inch thick. Cut with floured biscuit cutter without turning the biscuit cutter (push straight down) and place on a parchment-lined cookie sheet.

Bake for 12 to 15 minutes or until golden brown.

Makes 12 (2-inch) biscuits

Cinnamon Biscuits: Follow directions for Herbed Cheese Biscuits, omitting cheese and dill. Reduce the milk to ½ cup and sprinkle with a mixture of sugar and cinnamon. Bake at 425°F for 6 to 9 minutes or until golden brown.

honey whole-grain bread

3 cups whole wheat bread flour, divided

2 cups warm (not hot) whole milk

¾ to 1 cup all-purpose unbleached flour, divided

¼ cup honey

2 tablespoons vegetable oil

1 package active dry yeast

¾ teaspoon salt

helpful hint

To make foil handles, tear off three 18×2-inch strips of heavy foil or use regular foil folded to double thickness. Crisscross foil strips in spoke design and place in slow cooker to allow for easy removal of bread.

Slow Cooker Directions

1. Spray 1-quart casserole, soufflé dish or other high-sided baking pan that will fit in your slow cooker with nonstick cooking spray. Combine 1½ cups whole wheat flour, milk, ½ cup all-purpose flour, honey, oil, yeast and salt in large bowl. Beat with electric mixer at medium speed 2 minutes.

2. Add remaining 1½ cups whole wheat flour and ¼ cup to ½ cup all-purpose flour until dough is no longer sticky. (If mixer has difficulty mixing dough, mix in remaining flours with wooden spoon.) Transfer to prepared dish.

3. Make foil handles (see helpful hint). Place dish in slow cooker. Cover; cook on HIGH 3 hours or until edges are browned.

4. Use foil handles to lift dish from slow cooker. Let stand 5 minutes. Unmold on wire rack to cool.

Makes 8 to 10 servings

honey whole-grain bread

cheese corn muffins

½ cup corn meal

½ cup flour

¼ cup shredded JARLSBERG LITE™ Cheese

2 tablespoons sugar

1 tablespoon *each:* red and green bell peppers, minced

1 teaspoon baking powder

¾ teaspoon salt

½ cup plain non-fat yogurt

¼ cup (2 ounces) liquid egg substitute

2 tablespoons margarine, melted

Vegetable cooking spray

In medium bowl combine first 7 ingredients. In separate bowl, combine yogurt, egg substitute and margarine. Add dry ingredients to yogurt mixture and blend until evenly moistened. Spray muffin pan with vegetable cooking spray. Evenly divide batter to make 8 muffins. Bake at 400°F 15 to 20 minutes, until golden. Cool on wire rack 5 minutes. *Makes 8 muffins*

helpful hint

Muffins freeze well. Cool completely and place in a freezer-safe container.

cherry banana bread

- 1 (10-ounce) jar maraschino cherries
- 1¾ cups all-purpose flour
- 2 teaspoons baking powder
- ½ teaspoon salt
- ⅓ cup butter or margarine, softened
- ⅔ cup firmly packed brown sugar
- 2 eggs
- 1 cup mashed ripe bananas
- ½ cup chopped macadamia nuts or walnuts

Drain maraschino cherries, reserving 2 tablespoons juice. Cut cherries into quarters; set aside. Combine flour, baking powder and salt; set aside.

Combine butter, brown sugar, eggs and reserved cherry juice in a large mixing bowl. Mix with an electric mixer on medium speed 3 to 4 minutes, or until well mixed. Add flour mixture and mashed bananas alternately, beginning and ending with flour mixture. Stir in drained cherries and nuts. Lightly spray a 9×5×3-inch baking pan with non-stick cooking spray. Spread batter evenly in pan.

Bake in a preheated 350°F oven 1 hour, or until golden brown and wooden pick inserted near center comes out clean. Remove from pan; let cool on wire rack. To store, wrap bread in plastic wrap.

Makes 1 loaf (about 16 slices)

*Favorite recipe from **Cherry Marketing Institute***

cinnamon-pecan pull-apart bread

1½ cups water

¾ cup butter, divided

1 teaspoon salt

3¾ cups all-purpose flour

1¼ cups sugar, divided

2 teaspoons active dry yeast

¾ cup finely chopped pecans

1½ teaspoons ground cinnamon

½ cup raisins

Measuring carefully, place water, ¼ cup butter, salt, flour, ¼ cup sugar and yeast in bread machine pan in order specified by owner's manual. Program dough cycle setting; press start.

Melt remaining ½ cup butter. Combine remaining 1 cup sugar, pecans and cinnamon in small bowl. Divide dough in half; shape each half into twenty balls. Dip balls first in butter, then in sugar mixture. Arrange 20 balls in bottom of greased 12-cup tube pan; sprinkle with raisins. Top with remaining 20 balls. Cover and let rise in warm place 45 minutes or until doubled.

Preheat oven to 350°F. Bake 35 to 40 minutes or until evenly browned. Invert onto heatproof serving plate; let stand 1 minute before removing pan. Serve warm.

Makes 8 to 12 servings

orange bread

1 cup honey

2 tablespoons shortening

1 orange

1 egg, beaten

2⅔ cups all-purpose flour

2½ teaspoons baking powder

½ teaspoon salt

½ teaspoon baking soda

½ cup orange juice

¾ cup sliced blanched almonds

Preheat oven to 325°F. Grease 9×2-inch loaf pan. Set aside. Beat honey and shortening in large bowl with electric mixer. Grate orange rind to equal 1½ tablespoons. Peel, seed and chop remaining orange; set aside. Add egg and orange rind to honey mixture. Sift flour, baking powder, salt and baking soda into medium bowl. Add to honey mixture alternately with orange juice. Stir in orange and almonds. Pour batter into prepared pan. Bake 1 hour and 10 minutes or until toothpick inserted into center comes out clean.   *Makes 10 to 12 servings*

cinnamon-pecan pull-apart bread

easy crescents

1 cup warm water
(105°F to 115°F)

1 package (¼ ounce)
active dry yeast

5½ cups all-purpose flour,
divided

1 can (5⅓ ounces)
evaporated milk

⅓ cup sugar

2 large eggs, divided

1½ teaspoons salt

¼ cup butter or
margarine, melted
and cooled

1 cup cold butter or
margarine, cut into
¼-inch-thick slices

1 tablespoon cold water

1. Combine warm water and yeast in 1-quart bowl. Stir to dissolve yeast. Add 1 cup flour, evaporated milk, sugar, 1 egg and salt. Beat mixture with whisk to make smooth batter. Blend in melted butter. Reserve.

2. Fit processor with steel blade. Measure 3 cups flour and cold butter slices into work bowl. Process on/off 15 to 20 times until butter is in pieces no larger than kidney beans. Transfer mixture to large mixing bowl. Stir in remaining 1½ cups flour.

3. Pour yeast mixture over flour mixture. Stir with wooden spoon or rubber spatula just until all flour is moistened. Cover tightly and refrigerate until thoroughly chilled, at least 4 hours or up to 3 days.

4. Turn dough onto lightly floured surface. Knead about 6 times. Divide dough into 4 equal parts. Shape 1 part at a time, keeping others in refrigerator.

5. Roll each part on well-floured surface into circle about 17 inches in diameter. Cut into 8 equal pie-shaped wedges. Roll up each wedge starting at wide end and rolling towards point. Place on ungreased cookie sheets about 1½ inches apart. Curve ends of each roll to form crescent shapes.

6. Cover loosely with plastic wrap and let stand in warm place (85°F) until doubled in bulk, 1 to 1½ hours.

7. Heat oven to 325°F. Beat remaining egg and cold water with fork. Brush mixture over each roll. Bake until golden, 20 to 25 minutes. Remove immediately from cookie sheets to wire rack. Serve warm.

Makes 32 crescents

lemon raisin quick bread

1¼ cups all-purpose flour

¾ cup whole wheat flour

4 tablespoons sugar, divided

2 teaspoons baking powder

½ teaspoon baking soda

¼ teaspoon salt

1½ cups lemon-flavored low-fat yogurt

¼ cup unsalted butter, melted and cooled slightly

1 egg

½ teaspoon lemon peel

1 cup raisins

¾ cup chopped walnuts (optional)

Preheat oven to 350°F. Grease 8½×4½-inch loaf pan. Combine flours, 3 tablespoons sugar, baking powder, baking soda and salt in large bowl. Combine yogurt, butter, egg and lemon peel in medium bowl; stir until well blended. Pour yogurt mixture into flour mixture. Add raisins and walnuts, if desired; stir just until dry ingredients are moistened. Pour into prepared pan and smooth top. Sprinkle top with remaining 1 tablespoon sugar.

Bake 40 to 45 minutes or until lightly brown and toothpick inserted into center comes out clean. Cool in pan on wire rack 30 minutes. Remove from pan; cool completely. *Makes 1 loaf*

helpful hint

Quick breads require very little mixing or kneading and no rising time prior to baking. Bake these breads immediately after they are mixed so that leaveners do not lose their power.

green onion cream cheese breakfast biscuits

2 cups all-purpose flour

1 tablespoon baking powder

1 tablespoon sugar

¾ teaspoon salt

1 package (3 ounces) cream cheese

¼ cup shortening

½ cup finely chopped green onions

⅔ cup milk

helpful hint

When preparing biscuits, cut the shortening or butter into the dry ingredients with a pastry blender or two knives until the mixture forms coarse crumbs. Blending the fat in any further produces mealy biscuits. Mix the dough gently and quickly to achieve light and tender results. Overworking the dough makes the biscuits tough.

1. Preheat oven to 450°F.

2. Combine flour, baking powder, sugar and salt in medium bowl. Cut in cream cheese and shortening with pastry blender or two knives until mixture resembles coarse crumbs. Stir in green onions.

3. Make well in center of flour mixture. Add milk; stir until mixture forms soft dough that clings together and forms a ball.

4. Turn out dough onto well-floured surface. Knead dough gently 10 to 12 times.

5. Roll or pat dough to ½-inch thickness. Cut dough with floured 3-inch biscuit cutter.

6. Place biscuits 2 inches apart on ungreased large baking sheet. Bake 10 to 12 minutes or until tops and bottoms are golden brown. Serve warm.

Makes 8 biscuits

green onion cream cheese breakfast biscuits

SIDE DISH TIPS

A side dish is exactly what the name implies—a dish served beside a main entrée. Traditionally, thought to be vegetables, side dishes can also be anything from a simple salad to a creamy casserole. Side dishes should be fairly simply to make if you are investing a lot of time into your main dish. Choose flavors for the side dish that will complement the main dish well. For example, pair Asian Ginger Glazed Pork Chops (page 47) with Thai-Style Warm Noodle Salad (page 262). The flavors in both dishes will enhance each other. Too many different flavors in a meal will result in one strong flavor taking over the whole meal. Follow the tips below for making salads, choosing the right vegetables and cooking rice and pasta.

VEGETABLES

Preparation
Preparation can make or break the appeal of a vegetable. This is why it is important to know how cooking affects a vegetable's quality by changing its texture, flavor, color and nutrient content. If time is a problem when preparing vegetables, try using frozen or canned vegetables instead. This saves plenty of time and clean up is much easier.

Texture
Most raw vegetables are hard and fibrous, which makes them appropriate for dipping or salads. But if they are to accompany an entrée, they need to be softened to be palatable. Cooking softens the fiber in vegetables, making them more tender and easier to eat. The degree of tenderness is determined by how the vegetable is cut and how long it is cooked. Most vegetables are best when cooked to the crisp-tender stage.

Flavor
Some vegetable flavor is lost during cooking because flavor components leach into the

water and evaporate in the steam. The best way to avoid flavor loss is to cook vegetables in as little water as possible. With some strong-flavored vegetables, such as those in the cabbage family, it is desirable to dissolve some flavor into the cooking water or steam. Some freshly harvested vegetables, such as corn, peas and carrots, have a high sugar content that makes them taste sweet. As they mature or sit in storage, the sugar turns to starch, causing them to lose their sweetness. For the best flavor it is important to use fresh, seasonal vegetables.

Color
Cooking enhances the color of some vegetables, while overcooking can turn vibrant colors into dull grays and khaki greens. Because some pigments dissolve in water, such as those in beets and red cabbage, and others break down because of heat, such as those in peas and broccoli, vegetables should be cooked as quickly as possible to retain their colors.

Nutrient Content
Vegetables are important because they supply a wide assortment of nutrients. They are major sources of vitamins A and C and are loaded with other essential vitamins and minerals. However, a portion of these nutrients is lost during cooking—the larger the amount of water used, the higher the temperature and the longer the cooking time, the more nutrients the vegetables lose.

Purchase & Storage
Follow these purchasing tips and you can enjoy fresh vegetables at their peak flavor.

Asparagus: Choose firm, straight spears with closed, compact tips. The stalks should be crisp, not wilted, woody or dry. To store, stand the cut ends in an inch of water or wrap the ends in a moist paper towel. Place in a plastic bag in the refrigerator for up to five days.

Beans, Green/Peas: Look for vivid green, crisp beans without scars and well-shaped slim pods with small seeds. Avoid bruised or large beans or peas. To store, refrigerate, unwashed, in a plastic bag for up to two days.

Broccoli: Look for tightly closed, compact, dark green to purplish-green florets on firm yet tender stalks. Avoid those with yellow flowers, wilted leaves and tough stems. To store, refrigerate in a plastic bag for up to four days.

Cabbage: Look for well-trimmed, compact heads that feel heavy for their size. They should have a bright color and be free of withered leaves. Avoid cabbage with badly discolored or dry outer leaves. To store, refrigerate, unwashed, in a plastic bag for up to two weeks.

Carrots: Choose firm, well-shaped carrots with a deep orange color. Avoid those that are flabby, soft, cracked or shriveled. Some carrots come in bags or with the tops still on. Those with tops are often fresher. To store, cut the tops off. Refrigerate in a plastic bag for up to two days. Be sure to store carrots and apples separately, as apples produce a gas that causes carrots to develop a bitter flavor.

Corn: Choose corn with fresh, moist green husks; the cob should be well filled with bright, plump, milky kernels. Kernels should be tightly packed together in even rows. To store, refrigerate immediately in the husks. If shucked, store in plastic bags for up to two days. Use as soon as possible.

Eggplant: Look for a firm eggplant that is heavy for its size, with tight, glossy, deeply-colored skin. The stem should be bright green. Dull skin and rust-colored spots are signs of old age. To store, refrigerate, unwashed, in a plastic bag for up to five days.

Mushrooms, Button: Mushrooms should be firm and evenly colored with tightly closed caps. Avoid ones that are slimy or have any soft dark spots. To store, refrigerate in the original packaging for up to five days.

Onions: Choose firm, well-shaped onions with dry skins. Avoid those with sprouts. To store, place onions in a cool, dry, dark place up to one month, preferably hung where air can circulate around them. Do not refrigerate.

Peppers, Bell: Peppers should be firm, crisp and feel heavy for their size. They should be shiny and brightly colored, and their stems should be green and hard. Avoid those that have wrinkles, soft spots or bruises. To store, refrigerate, unwashed, for up to three days. Green peppers can be stored slightly longer than red or yellow peppers.

Potatoes: Choose potatoes that are well-shaped, firm and relatively smooth. Avoid green-colored or tinged potatoes and those with sprouts. The "eyes" should be few and shallow. Store potatoes in a cool, dry, dark place for up to two weeks. (New potatoes should be eaten within three days of purchase.) Check them occasionally and remove any potatoes that have sprouted or begun to shrivel. One rotten potato can spoil the whole lot. Avoid storing potatoes and onions together as the gases given off by the onions can cause the potatoes to spoil more quickly.

Squash, Summer: Choose small to medium-size squash (no longer than 8 inches) that are firm with smooth, glossy, unblemished skins. They should feel heavy for their size. To store, refrigerate, unwashed, in a perforated plastic bag for up to four days. Yellow squash and zucchini are the two most common types of summer squash.

Tomatoes: Look for tomatoes that are plump and heavy with a vibrant color and a pleasant aroma. They should be firm but not hard. Avoid those that are cracked or have soft spots. Tomatoes should never be refrigerated before cutting, because cold temperatures cause their flesh to become mealy and lose flavor.

SIDE DISH TIPS

RICE

Rice is the staple food of half of the world's population. There are three commercial grades of rice: long, medium and short grain. Long-grain rice kernels are a good choice for pilafs and rice salads. Medium-grain rice is perfect for croquettes and molded dishes. Short-grain rice can be used for risotto, rice pudding and other sweet rice dishes.

Store rice in an airtight container in a cool, dry place. It will keep indefinitely. Brown rice is subject to rancidity because the bran is intact. It can be stored for only six months. It is not necessary to rinse most rice before cooking. However, basmati rice may contain some chaff and small stones. Remove any debris before cooking and rinse, if necessary.

Cooking Rice

Rice has a reputation for being difficult to cook. Since rice can be cooked by several methods, the choice is dependent upon the result you desire. To prepare brown, converted, flavored or quick-cooking rices, follow the package directions. The most common cooking methods for polished white rice are the boiling method, the most used method, and the pilaf method, used to make rice that is sticky.

PASTA

Pasta is an Italian word that describes all the various products made with wheat flour and water, such as spaghetti, macaroni, penne and noodles.

Cooking Pasta

As a general rule, 2 ounces of dry pasta is equal to a first-course or side-dish serving. Use 3 to 4 ounces dry pasta per person for each main-dish serving. Spaghetti and macaroni products usually double in amount when cooked, but egg noodles do not expand significantly. Fresh pasta is much moister and does not expand, so use 3 ounces of fresh pasta for each side-dish serving and 4 to 5 ounces for each main-dish serving.

A faster cooking time makes fresh pasta more convenient than dried; fresh pasta usually cooks in 3 minutes or less, depending on the desired doneness, while dried pasta requires 7 to 12 minutes cooking time. When substituting dried pasta for fresh, make sure to allow extra cooking time.

SENSATIONAL SIDE DISHES

······································

southwestern potato salad

5 large red or white boiling potatoes (about 2 pounds total)

Boiling water

¼ **pound bacon**

½ **cup canned diced green chilies, drained**

⅓ **cup chopped fresh parsley**

¼ **cup finely chopped onion**

⅓ **cup vegetable oil**

3 **tablespoons white wine vinegar**

½ **teaspoon salt**

¼ **teaspoon black pepper**

¼ **teaspoon ground cumin**

3 **drops hot pepper sauce**

Place potatoes in large saucepan with 2 inches of boiling water. Cook, covered, 20 to 25 minutes or until tender. Drain and let stand until cool. Meanwhile, place bacon in large skillet; cook over medium-high heat until crisp. Drain bacon on paper towels. Let cool slightly; crumble. Cut potatoes into cubes; place in large bowl. Add bacon, chilies, parsley and onion; mix lightly. Whisk remaining ingredients in small bowl until well blended. Pour over potato mixture; toss gently to coat potatoes evenly. Cover and refrigerate 2 hours for flavors to blend.

Makes 6 to 8 servings

southwestern potato salad

cold asparagus with lemon-mustard dressing

12 fresh asparagus spears

2 tablespoons fat-free mayonnaise

1 tablespoon sweet brown mustard

1 tablespoon fresh lemon juice

1 teaspoon grated lemon peel, divided

1. Steam asparagus until crisp-tender and bright green; immediately drain and rinse under cold water. Cover and refrigerate until chilled.

2. Combine mayonnaise, mustard and lemon juice in small bowl; blend well. Stir in ½ teaspoon lemon peel; set aside.

3. Divide asparagus between 2 plates. Spoon 2 tablespoons dressing over top of each serving; sprinkle each with ¼ teaspoon lemon peel. Garnish with carrot strips and edible flowers, such as pansies, violets or nasturtiums, if desired. *Makes 2 appetizer servings*

lemony steamed broccoli

1 pound broccoli

1 tablespoon butter

2 teaspoons lemon juice

Salt and black pepper

1. Break broccoli into florets. Discard large stems. Trim smaller stems; cut stems into thin slices.

2. Place 2 to 3 inches of water and steamer basket in large saucepan; bring water to a boil.

3. Add broccoli; cover. Steam 6 minutes or until crisp-tender.

4. Place broccoli in serving bowl. Add butter and lemon juice; toss lightly to coat. Season with salt and pepper to taste. *Makes 4 servings*

cold asparagus with lemon-mustard dressing

thai peanut salad

1 cup picante sauce

¼ cup chunky-style peanut butter

2 tablespoons honey

2 tablespoons orange juice

1 teaspoon soy sauce

½ teaspoon ground ginger

2 cups (12 ounces) chopped CURE 81® ham

1 (7-ounce) package spaghetti, cooked

¼ cup dry roasted unsalted peanuts

¼ cup red bell pepper, cut into julienne strips

2 tablespoons chopped cilantro

In small saucepan, combine picante sauce, peanut butter, honey, orange juice, soy sauce and ginger. Cook, stirring over low heat until mixture is smooth. Add ¼ cup sauce mixture to ham. Gently toss remaining sauce mixture with hot cooked pasta. Toss pasta mixture with ham mixture, peanuts and pepper strips. Cover and chill 1 to 2 hours. Before serving, sprinkle with cilantro. *Makes 4 servings*

thai peanut salad

oven-roasted potatoes

2 large baking potatoes (about 10 ounces each)

2 tablespoons butter or margarine, melted

2 tablespoons vegetable oil

Salt and black pepper

1. Preheat oven to 425°F.

2. Scrub potatoes; do not peel. Thinly slice potatoes crosswise. Pat potato slices dry with paper towels.

3. Place potatoes in medium bowl. Add butter and oil; toss to coat. Place on nonstick baking sheet.

4. Bake 10 minutes or until tender and lightly browned, stirring lightly after 5 minutes. Season with salt and pepper to taste. *Makes 4 servings*

green bean casserole

1 can (10¾ ounces) condensed cream of mushroom soup

¾ cup milk

⅛ teaspoon ground black pepper

2 packages (9 ounces each) frozen cut green beans, thawed and drained *or* 2 cans (14½ ounces each) cut green beans, drained

1⅓ cups *French's*® French Fried Onions, divided

Preheat oven to 350°F. Combine soup, milk and ground pepper in 1½-quart casserole; stir until well blended. Stir in beans and ⅔ *cup* French Fried Onions.

Bake, uncovered, 30 minutes or until hot. Stir; sprinkle with remaining ⅔ *cup* onions. Bake 5 minutes or until onions are golden. *Makes 6 servings*

Microwave Directions: Prepare green bean mixture as above. Pour into 1½-quart microwavable casserole. Cover loosely with plastic wrap. Microwave on HIGH 8 to 10 minutes or until heated through, stirring halfway through cooking time. Uncover; sprinkle with remaining onions. Cook 1 minute or until onions are golden. Let stand 5 minutes.

Prep Time: 5 minutes
Cook Time: 35 minutes

cottage fried potatoes

Canola oil

3 to 4 russet potatoes (about 1½ pounds), cut into wedges

Coarse salt

Add a little kick to these potatoes by seasoning them with ¼ teaspoon chili powder or paprika.

1. Preheat oven to 250°F. Line 2 large baking sheets with paper towels; set aside.

2. Pour oil into large deep skillet or wok to 1-inch depth. Attach deep-fry or candy thermometer to side of skillet, making sure bulb is submerged in oil but not touching bottom of skillet. Heat oil over high heat until thermometer registers 390°F.

3. Carefully slide 8 to 10 potato wedges into skillet. (Do not crowd skillet or oil will lose too much heat.) Reduce heat to medium-high; cook about 4 minutes or until potatoes are deep golden brown and skins are crispy, turning gently to separate wedges so that they cook evenly.

4. Carefully remove potatoes and arrange in single layer on baking sheet. Blot excess oil from potatoes. Place baking sheet in oven to keep potatoes warm.

5. Repeat steps 2 through 4 with remaining potatoes. Sprinkle potatoes with salt to taste. Serve hot.

Makes 4 to 6 servings

cottage fried potatoes

vegetable couscous

3 cups water

**1 package KNORR®
Recipe Classics™
Vegetable Soup, Dip
and Recipe Mix**

**2 tablespoons
BERTOLLI® Olive
Oil or I CAN'T
BELIEVE IT'S NOT
BUTTER!® Spread**

**1 package (10 ounces)
plain couscous
(about 1½ cups)**

**¼ cup chopped fresh
parsley (optional)**

**Pine nuts, slivered
almonds or raisins
(optional)**

• In 2-quart saucepan, bring water, recipe mix and olive oil to a boil, stirring frequently. Reduce heat; cover and simmer 2 minutes.

• Stir couscous into saucepan until evenly moistened. Remove from heat; cover and let stand 5 minutes.

• Fluff couscous with fork. Spoon into serving dish. Garnish, if desired, with chopped parsley and nuts or raisins. *Makes 5 cups couscous*

Recipe Tip: Turn Vegetable Couscous into an easy one-dish meal. Just add 2 cups cut-up cooked chicken or turkey to the saucepan in step 1.

Prep Time: 5 minutes
Cook Time: 10 minutes

vegetable couscous

broccoli with creamy lemon sauce

2 tablespoons fat-free
    mayonnaise

1 tablespoon plus
    1½ teaspoons
    reduced-fat sour
    cream

1 tablespoon fat-free
    (skim) milk

1 to 1½ teaspoons
    lemon juice

⅛ teaspoon ground
    turmeric

1¼ cups hot cooked
    broccoli florets

Combine all ingredients except broccoli in top of double boiler. Cook over simmering water 5 minutes or until heated through, stirring constantly. Serve over hot cooked broccoli.   *Makes 2 servings*

helpful hint

Turmeric is a spice widely used in Indian cooking. It has a pungent flavor and yellowish color and can be found in most supermarket spice sections.

cole slaw vinaigrette

¼ cup vegetable oil

2 tablespoons white
    wine vinegar

1 tablespoon honey

    Salt and black pepper

1 (8-ounce) package
    cole slaw mix

1. Whisk together oil, vinegar and honey. Season with salt and pepper to taste.

2. Place cole slaw mix in medium bowl.

3. Pour vinaigrette over cole slaw mix. Toss lightly to coat; cover. Refrigerate.   *Makes 4 servings*

broccoli with creamy lemon sauce

broiled zucchini halves

½ cup (2 ounces)
    shredded mozzarella
    cheese

2 tablespoons diced
    pimiento

2 tablespoons chopped
    ripe olives

4 small zucchini (about
    1 pound total),
    sliced lengthwise

1 tablespoon olive oil

1. Preheat broiler; place oven rack 6 inches below heat source. Combine cheese, pimiento and olives in small bowl; set aside.

2. Brush both sides of zucchini halves with oil; arrange on broiler pan lined with foil. Broil 5 minutes or until fork-tender.

3. Spoon about 2 tablespoons cheese mixture along each zucchini half. Broil until cheese melts and browns. Serve immediately.   *Makes 4 side-dish servings*

Prep and Cook Time: 15 minutes

helpful hint

Choose zucchini that are heavy for their size, firm and well shaped. They should have a bright color and be free of cuts and any soft spots. Small zucchini are more tender because they have been harvested when they were young.

broiled zucchini halves

mexicali corn

1 tablespoon butter or margarine

1½ cups chopped onion and bell pepper

1 package (16 ounces) frozen whole kernel corn

⅛ teaspoon garlic powder

3 tablespoons *Frank's®* *RedHot®* Original Cayenne Pepper Sauce

1. Melt butter in saucepan over medium-high heat. Cook and stir onion and peppers in butter until crisp-tender. Stir in corn and garlic powder.

2. Cover pan; cook over medium heat 3 minutes until corn is tender. Stir in **Frank's RedHot** Sauce.

Makes 4 to 6 servings

Prep Time: 5 minutes
Cook Time: 8 minutes

sautéed zucchini and yellow squash

5 tablespoons unsalted butter

2 teaspoons Chef Paul Prudhomme's Vegetable Magic®

1 cup chopped onion

2 cups thinly sliced yellow squash*

2 cups thinly sliced zucchini*

You may substitute cauliflower, carrots, broccoli or other vegetables of your choice for all or part of the squashes.

Melt the butter in a large skillet over high heat. Add the Vegetable Magic and stir until well blended. Add the onion and sauté until golden brown, about 5 minutes, stirring occasionally and scraping pan bottom well. Add the squashes and cook until somewhat tender but still crispy, about 2 minutes, stirring frequently and being sure that all of the vegetable slices are well coated with the butter. Serve immediately.

Makes 2 to 3 servings

grilled sweet potatoes

4 medium-sized sweet potatoes (2 pounds), peeled

⅓ cup *French's*® Honey Dijon Mustard

2 tablespoons olive oil

1 tablespoon minced fresh rosemary *or* 1 teaspoon dried rosemary

½ teaspoon salt

¼ teaspoon black pepper

1. Cut potatoes diagonally into ½-inch-thick slices. Place potatoes and 1 cup water in shallow microwavable dish. Cover with vented plastic wrap and microwave on HIGH (100%) 6 minutes or until potatoes are crisp-tender, turning once. (Cook potatoes in two batches, if necessary.) Drain well.

2. Combine mustard, oil, rosemary, salt and pepper in small bowl; brush on potato slices. Place potatoes on oiled grid. Grill over medium-high heat 5 to 8 minutes or until potatoes are fork-tender, turning and basting often with mustard mixture. *Makes 4 servings*

Tip: The task of selecting sweet potatoes is an easy one. Just look for medium-sized potatoes with thick, dark orange skins that are free from bruises. Sweet potatoes keep best in a dry, dark area at about 55°F. Under these conditions they should last about 3 to 4 weeks.

Prep Time: 15 minutes
Cook Time: 18 minutes

grilled sweet potatoes

pasta waldorf

8 ounces uncooked small shell pasta

2 red delicious apples, peeled, cored and diced

1 rib celery, chopped

½ cup chopped pecans

½ cup chopped raisins

⅓ cup nonfat lemon yogurt

⅓ cup reduced-fat mayonnaise

Salt

1. Cook pasta according to package directions; drain. Rinse in cold water; drain again.

2. Combine pasta, apples, celery, pecans, raisins, yogurt and mayonnaise in large bowl. Toss gently until blended. Season to taste with salt. Cover and chill 5 minutes.   *Makes 6 side-dish servings*

Prep/Cook/Chill Time: 20 minutes

oven-roasted asparagus

1 bunch (12 to 14 ounces) asparagus spears

1 tablespoon olive oil

½ teaspoon salt

¼ teaspoon ground black pepper

¼ cup shredded Asiago or Parmesan cheese

1. Preheat oven to 425°F.

2. Trim off and discard tough ends of asparagus spears. Peel stem ends of asparagus with vegetable peeler, if desired. Arrange asparagus in shallow baking dish. Drizzle oil onto asparagus; turn spears to coat. Sprinkle with salt and pepper.

3. Bake until asparagus is tender, about 12 to 18 minutes depending on thickness of asparagus. Chop or leave spears whole. Sprinkle with cheese.

Makes 4 servings

pasta waldorf

vegetable-stuffed baked potatoes

1 jar (1 pound) RAGÚ®
Cheese Creations!®
Roasted Garlic
Parmesan Sauce or
Double Cheddar
Sauce

1 bag (16 ounces) frozen
assorted vegetables,
cooked and drained

6 large baking potatoes,
unpeeled and baked

In 2-quart saucepan, heat Ragú Cheese Creations!
Roasted Garlic Parmesan Sauce. Stir in vegetables; heat
through.

Cut a lengthwise slice from top of each potato. Lightly
mash pulp in each potato. Evenly spoon sauce mixture
onto each potato. Sprinkle, if desired, with ground
black pepper. *Makes 6 servings*

vegetable-stuffed baked potato

sesame-honey vegetable casserole

1 package (16 ounces) frozen mixed vegetable medley, such as baby carrots, broccoli, onions and red peppers, thawed and drained

3 tablespoons honey

1 tablespoon dark sesame oil

1 tablespoon soy sauce

2 teaspoons sesame seeds

1. Preheat oven to 350°F. Place vegetables in shallow, 1½-quart casserole dish or quiche pan.

2. Combine remaining ingredients; mix well. Drizzle evenly over vegetables. Bake 20 to 25 minutes or until vegetables are hot, stirring after 15 minutes.

Makes 4 to 6 servings

helpful hint

Sesame seeds are widely available packaged in supermarkets and are sold in bulk in specialty stores and ethnic markets. Because of their high oil content, they easily turn rancid and are best stored in the refrigerator where they will keep up to six months or they may be frozen up to a year.

chicken salad with BelGioioso® mascarpone

8 ounces cooked chicken chunks

1 teaspoon Dijon mustard

2 tablespoons mayonnaise or salad dressing

Dash garlic salt

Dash dill seasoning

2½ tablespoons BELGIOIOSO® Mascarpone

1 tomato (cut in wedges)

Mix chicken, mustard, salad dressing, garlic salt, dill seasoning and BelGioioso Mascarpone together in a bowl (use seasoning to taste). Garnish with tomato wedges and serve on a bed of mix greens.

Makes 4 to 6 servings

herbed corn on the cob

1 tablespoon butter or
   margarine
1 teaspoon mixed dried
   herb leaves, such as
   basil, oregano, sage
   and rosemary
⅛ teaspoon salt
   Black pepper
4 ears corn, husks
   removed

Microwave Directions

1. Combine butter, herbs, salt and pepper in small microwavable bowl. Microwave at MEDIUM (50%) 30 to 45 seconds or until butter is melted.

2. With pastry brush, coat corn with butter mixture. Place corn on microwavable plate; microwave at HIGH 5 to 6 minutes. Turn corn over and microwave at HIGH 5 to 6 minutes until tender.   *Makes 4 servings*

The Original Ranch® roasted potatoes

2 pounds small red
   potatoes, quartered
¼ cup vegetable oil
1 packet (1 ounce)
   **HIDDEN VALLEY®
   The Original Ranch®
   Salad Dressing &
   Seasoning Mix**

Place potatoes in a resealable plastic bag and add oil; seal bag. Toss to coat. Add salad dressing & seasoning mix and toss again until coated. Bake in an ungreased baking pan at 450°F for 35 minutes or until potatoes are brown and crisp.   *Makes 4 to 6 servings*

herbed corn on the cob

thai-style warm noodle salad

8 ounces uncooked angel hair pasta

½ cup chunky peanut butter

¼ cup soy sauce

¼ to ½ teaspoon red pepper flakes

2 green onions, thinly sliced

1 carrot, shredded

helpful hint

This salad is as versatile as it is easy to make. It can be prepared a day ahead and served warm or cold—perfect for potlucks, picnics and even lunch boxes. You can also make it into a heartier meal by mixing in any leftover chicken or beef.

1. Cook pasta according to package directions.

2. While pasta is cooking, blend peanut butter, soy sauce and red pepper flakes in serving bowl until smooth.

3. Drain pasta, reserving 5 tablespoons water. Mix hot pasta water with peanut butter mixture until smooth; toss pasta with sauce. Stir in green onions and carrot. Serve warm or at room temperature.

Makes 4 serving

Prep and Cook Time: 12 minutes

thai-style warm noodle salad

DESSERTS DIVULGED

Dessert—the grand finale to any meal—does not have to be extravagant or take you hours to make. The goal is to make it look and taste like it has taken hours to make! The dessert recipes that follow on pages 268 to 309 will help you accomplish this goal.

The word dessert is a very broad term. It can mean cookies, brownies, cakes, pies, puddings and so much more. Below you will find some quick tips and information on some of the desserts featured in this chapter.

COOKIES
The seemingly endless variety of cookies can actually be divided into five basic types: bar, drop, refrigerator, rolled and shaped. These types are determined by the consistency of the dough and how it is formed into cookies.

Cookie Dough
• Cookies that are uniform in size and shape will finish baking at the same time. To easily shape drop cookies into a uniform size, use an ice cream scoop with a release bar. The bar usually has a number on it indicating the number of scoops that can be made from one quart of ice cream. The handiest sizes for cookies are a #50 and #80 scoop. They make 2- or 3-inch cookies.

• Always shape dough for refrigerator cookies into rolls before chilling. Shaping is easier if you first place the dough on a piece of waxed paper or plastic wrap. Before chilling, wrap the rolls securely in plastic wrap so that air cannot penetrate the dough and cause it to dry out.

• Use gentle pressure and a back-and-forth sawing motion when slicing refrigerator cookie dough so that the cookies will have a nice round shape. Rotating the roll while slicing also prevents one side from getting flat.

• For easier handling, chill cookie dough for cutouts before rolling. Remove only enough dough from the refrigerator to work with at one time. Save any trimmings and reroll them all at once to prevent the dough from becoming tough.

• Unbaked dough can be refrigerated for up to two weeks or frozen for up to six weeks. Rolls of dough should be wrapped tightly in plastic wrap; other doughs should be stored in airtight containers. Label the dough with baking information for convenience.

Cookie Sheets
Not all cookie sheets are created equal. Here are a few guidelines for using cookie sheets and pans.

• The best cookie sheets to use are those with little or no sides. They allow the heat to circulate easily during baking and promote even browning.

• Use shiny cookie sheets for the best cookie baking results. Dark cookie sheets will cause the bottoms of the cookies to be dark. Insulated baking sheets have a layer of air sandwiched between two sheets of aluminum which helps to prevent excess browning but increases baking time. (Some cookie doughs may also spread more on these sheets.) Using this type of cookie sheet may not yield crisp cookies.

• When making bar cookies or brownies, use the pan size specified in the recipe and prepare the pans according to the recipe directions.

• When a recipe calls for greasing, use shortening or vegetable cooking spray for the best results. Lining the cookie sheets with parchment paper is an alternative to greasing. It eliminates clean-up, allows the cookies to bake more evenly and cool right on the paper instead of on wire racks.

• For even baking and browning, place only one cookie sheet at a time in the center of the oven. If the heat distribution in your oven is uneven, turn the cookie sheet halfway through the baking time. Also, if you do use more than one sheet at a time, rotate the cookie sheets from top to bottom halfway through the baking time.

• Allow cookie sheets to cool between batches; the dough will spread if placed on a hot cookie sheet.

Storing and Freezing
• Store soft and crisp cookies separately at room temperature to prevent changes in texture and flavor.

• Keep soft cookies in airtight containers. If they begin to dry out, add a piece of apple or bread to the container to help them retain moisture.

• Store crisp cookies in containers with loose-fitting lids to prevent moisture build-up.

If they become soggy, heat undecorated cookies in a 300°F oven for 3 to 5 minutes to restore crispness.

• Store cookies with sticky glazes, fragile decorations and icings in single layers between sheets of waxed paper.

• Bar cookies and brownies may be stored in their own baking pan, covered with foil or plastic wrap when cool.

• As a rule, crisp cookies freeze better than soft, moist cookies. Rich, buttery bar cookies and brownies are an exception to this rule since they freeze extremely well.

• Freeze baked cookies in airtight containers or freezer bags for up to six months.

• Thaw cookies and brownies unwrapped at room temperature.

• Meringue-based cookies do not freeze well, and chocolate-dipped cookies will discolor if frozen.

CAKES

Cakes are generally divided into two broad groups based on how they are leavened: chemically leavened (shortened) and air-leavened (foam) cakes.

Baking

After filling the cake pan, immediately place it in the center of a preheated oven. Cake batter should not sit before baking, because chemical leaveners begin working as soon as they are mixed with liquids or because the air in foam batters will begin to dissipate. Oven racks may need to be set lower for cakes baked in tube pans. If two racks are used, arrange them so they divide the oven into thirds and then stagger the pans so they are not directly over each other. Avoid opening the oven door during the first half of the baking time. The oven temperature must remain constant in order for the cake to rise properly.

Cooling

Many cakes are removed from the pan after 10 to 15 minutes of cooling on a wire rack. Two important exceptions are angel food cakes and flourless cakes. Because they have a more delicate structure, they are cooled in the pan. Angel food cakes and some chiffon cakes are cooled in the pan upside down. An angel food cake pan has three metal feet on which the inverted pan stands for cooling. If you use a tube pan instead, invert the pan on a funnel or narrow-necked bottle.

Before attempting to remove a cake from its pan, carefully run a table knife or narrow metal spatula around the outside of the cake to loosen it from the pan. Using oven mitts or hot pads (if the pan is hot), place a wire cooling rack on top of the cake and pan. Turn the cake over so that the wire rack is on the bottom. Gently shake the cake to release it from the pan. Place the rack on a counter and remove the pan.

PIES

A pie is a sweet or savory baked dish with a crust and a filling. Dessert pies may be baked or chilled. They are usually made in a pie pan. They feature a variety of crusts made from pastry dough or graham cracker or cookie crumbs.

•Chiffon pies are single-crust chilled pies with a light, airy filling made by folding whipped cream or stiffly beaten egg whites into a gelatin-, cream- or cream cheese-based mixture.

•Cream pies are single-crust chilled pies with a rich, sweet puddinglike filling. They are usually topped with meringue, whipped cream or fruit.

•Custard pies are single-crust baked pies with a sweet, rich custard filling made from eggs and milk.

•Frozen pies have a single crust. They are filled with an ice cream, cream cheese or chiffon filling.

•Fruit pies may have single or double crusts. They are filled with fresh, canned or frozen fruit and baked.

CHEESECAKES

Cheesecake is a creamy baked dessert made from cream cheese or ricotta cheese that is sweetened and flavored. The texture can range from airy and light to dense and heavy. Some are flawlessly smooth and moist while others have a drier and more crumbly consistency. A picture-perfect cheesecake has a smooth top. Some cheesecakes will have a narrow crack around the rim; wide center cracks are unattractive.

OTHER DESSERTS

•Baked in a casserole or baking dish, cobblers are similar to deep-dish pies, but have a rich, thick biscuit topping. Cobblers are often served warm with vanilla ice cream or whipped cream.

•A crisp is a baked fruit dessert topped with a crisp, crunchy topping. Fruit is first placed in the dish and then a crumbled topping, usually flour, sugar and butter, is sprinkled over the top. The dessert is then baked and the crumb topping becomes crisp. Crisps are often topped with whipped cream or ice cream and are best served warm.

•A trifle is a layered dessert of English origin. It begins with a layer of ladyfingers or sponge cake pieces that are sprinkled with sherry or another liquor, spread with jam and topped with custard. The layers are usually repeated. It is refrigerated for several hours before serving to allow the flavors to blend. A trifle is generally served in a glass bowl to display the layers. Just before serving, it is topped with whipped cream.

DECADENT DESSERTS

fudgy milk chocolate fondue

1 (16-ounce) can chocolate-flavored syrup

1 (14-ounce) can EAGLE BRAND® Sweetened Condensed Milk (NOT evaporated milk)

Dash salt

1½ teaspoons vanilla extract

Assorted dippers: cookies, cake cubes, pound cake cubes, angel food cake cubes, banana chunks, apple slices, strawberries, pear slices, kiwifruit slices and/or marshmallows

1. In heavy saucepan over medium heat, combine syrup, Eagle Brand and salt. Cook and stir 12 to 15 minutes or until slightly thickened.

2. Remove from heat; stir in vanilla. Serve warm with assorted dippers. Store covered in refrigerator.

Makes about 3 cups

Microwave Directions: In 1-quart glass measure, combine syrup, Eagle Brand and salt. Microwave at HIGH (100% power) 3½ to 4 minutes, stirring after 2 minutes. Stir in vanilla.

Tip: Can be served warm or cold over ice cream. Can be made several weeks ahead. Store tightly covered in refrigerator.

Prep Time: 12 to 15 minutes

fudgy milk chocolate fondue

white chocolate pudding parfaits

1 package (4-serving size) sugar-free instant white chocolate pudding mix

2 cups low-fat (2%) milk

¾ cup whipping cream

1½ cups fresh raspberries or sliced strawberries

2 tablespoons chopped roasted shelled pistachio nuts or chopped toasted macadamia nuts

1. Add pudding mix to milk; beat with wire whisk or electric mixer 2 minutes. Refrigerate 5 minutes or until thickened. Beat whipping cream in small deep bowl with electric mixer at high speed until stiff peaks form. Fold whipped cream into pudding.

2. In each of 4 parfait or wine glasses, layer ¼ cup pudding and 2 tablespoons raspberries. Repeat layers. Spoon remaining pudding over berries. Serve immediately or cover and chill up to 6 hours before serving. Just before serving, sprinkle with nuts.

Makes 4 servings

flourless peanut butter cookies

1 cup peanut butter

1 cup packed light brown sugar

1 egg

24 milk chocolate candy stars or other solid milk chocolate candy

Preheat oven to 350°F. Combine peanut butter, sugar and egg in medium bowl; beat until blended and smooth.

Shape dough into 24 balls about 1½ inches in diameter. Place 2 inches apart on ungreased cookie sheets. Press one chocolate star on top of each cookie. Bake 10 to 12 minutes or until set. Transfer to wire racks to cool completely.

Makes about 2 dozen cookies

white chocolate pudding parfaits

lazy-daisy cake

2 cups granulated sugar

4 eggs

½ cup (1 stick) butter, softened and divided

2 teaspoons vanilla

2 cups all-purpose flour

2 teaspoons baking powder

1 cup warm milk

1 cup coconut flakes

½ cup plus 2 tablespoons packed brown sugar

⅓ cup half-and-half

1. Preheat oven to 350°F. Grease 13×9-inch baking pan.

2. Beat granulated sugar, eggs, 2 tablespoons butter and vanilla 3 minutes in large bowl with electric mixer at medium speed until fluffy. Sift flour and baking powder into medium bowl. Beat into egg mixture until well blended. Stir in milk and 2 tablespoons butter. Pour into prepared pan. Bake 30 minutes or until toothpick inserted into center comes out clean.

3. Meanwhile, combine remaining 4 tablespoons butter, coconut, brown sugar and half-and-half in medium saucepan over medium heat. Cook until sugar dissolves and butter melts, stirring constantly.

4. Spread coconut mixture over warm cake. Place under broiler, 4 inches from heat source. Broil 2 to 3 minutes or until top turns light golden brown.

Makes 12 to 14 servings

lazy-daisy cake

double chocolate brownies

1¼ cups all-purpose flour, divided

¼ cup sugar

½ cup (1 stick) cold butter or margarine

1 (14-ounce) can EAGLE BRAND® Sweetened Condensed Milk (NOT evaporated milk)

¼ cup unsweetened cocoa

1 egg

1 teaspoon vanilla extract

½ teaspoon baking powder

1 (8-ounce) milk chocolate bar, broken into chunks

¾ cup chopped nuts, if desired

1. Preheat oven to 350°F. Line 13×9-inch baking pan with foil; set aside.

2. In medium mixing bowl, combine 1 cup flour and sugar; cut in butter until crumbly. Press firmly on bottom of prepared pan. Bake 15 minutes.

3. In large bowl, beat Eagle Brand, cocoa, egg, remaining ¼ cup flour, vanilla and baking powder. Stir in chocolate chunks and nuts, if desired. Spread over baked crust. Bake 20 minutes or until set.

4. Cool. Use foil to lift out of pan. Cut into bars. Store tightly covered at room temperature.

Makes 24 brownies

Prep Time: 15 minutes
Bake Time: 35 minutes

creamy lemon cheesecake

9 graham crackers,
  crushed into crumbs

⅓ cup blanched
  almonds, ground

6 tablespoons butter or
  margarine, melted

¾ cup plus 2 tablespoons
  sugar, divided

3 packages (8 ounces
  each) cream cheese,
  softened

1 container (15 ounces)
  ricotta cheese

4 eggs, lightly beaten

2 tablespoons finely
  grated lemon peel

1 teaspoon lemon
  extract

1 teaspoon vanilla

Preheat oven to 375°F.

Blend graham cracker crumbs, almonds, butter and
2 tablespoons sugar in small bowl. Press evenly on
bottom and ½ inch up side of 9-inch springform pan.
Bake 5 minutes. Remove; cool pan on wire rack. *Reduce
oven to 325°F.*

Combine cream cheese, ricotta cheese, eggs, remaining
¾ cup sugar, lemon peel, lemon extract and vanilla
in large bowl. Beat with electric mixer at low speed
until blended. Increase mixer speed to high. Beat 4 to
5 minutes until smooth and creamy. Pour into prepared
crust.

Bake 1 hour and 10 minutes or until just set in center.
Do not overbake. Cool to room temperature on wire rack.
Cover and refrigerate at least four hours or overnight.

Makes 12 servings

creamy lemon cheesecake

peanut butter surprise cookies

24 miniature peanut
    butter cups

1 can (14 ounces)
    sweetened
    condensed milk (not
    evaporated milk)

¾ cup JIF® Creamy
    Peanut Butter

¼ Butter Flavor
    CRISCO® Stick or
    ¼ cup Butter Flavor
    CRISCO® all-
    vegetable
    shortening

1 egg

1 teaspoon vanilla

2 cups regular all-
    purpose baking mix

1. Remove wrappers from peanut butter cups. Cut candy into quarters.

2. Combine condensed milk, peanut butter, ¼ cup shortening, egg and vanilla in large bowl. Beat at medium speed of electric mixer until smooth. Add baking mix. Beat until well blended. Stir in candy pieces with spoon. Cover. Refrigerate 1 hour.

3. Heat oven to 350°F. Place sheets of foil on countertop for cooling cookies.

4. Drop dough by slightly rounded teaspoonfuls 2 inches apart onto ungreased baking sheet. Shape into balls with spoon.

5. Bake at 350°F for 7 to 9 minutes or until light brown around edges and center is just set. *Do not overbake.* Cool 2 minutes on baking sheet. Remove cookies to foil to cool completely.　　*Makes about 4 dozen cookies*

Variation: Shape dough into 1¼-inch balls. Place 2 inches apart onto ungreased baking sheet. Dip fork in flour; flatten dough slightly in crisscross pattern.

peanut butter surprise cookies

apple-gingerbread mini cakes

1 large Cortland or
 Jonathan apple,
 cored and quartered

1 package (14½ ounces)
 gingerbread cake
 and cookie mix

1 cup water

1 egg

 Powdered sugar
 (optional)

Microwave Directions

1. Lightly grease 10 (6- to 7-ounce) custard cups; set aside. Grate apple in food processor or with hand-held grater. Combine grated apple, cake mix, water and egg in medium bowl; stir until well blended. Spoon about ⅓ cup mix into each custard cup, filling cups ½ full.

2. Arrange 5 cups in microwave. Microwave at HIGH 2 minutes. Rotate cups ½ turn. Microwave 1 minute more or until cakes are springy when touched and look slightly moist on top. Cool on wire rack. Repeat with remaining cakes.

3. To unmold cakes, run a small knife around edge of custard cups to loosen cakes while still warm. Invert on cutting board and tap lightly until cake drops out. Place on plates. When cool enough, dust with powdered sugar, if desired. Serve warm or at room temperature.

Makes 10 cakes

Serving Suggestion: Serve with vanilla ice cream, whipped cream or crème anglaise.

Prep and Cook Time: 20 minutes

apple-gingerbread mini cake

pineapple upside-down cake

¼ cup plus 2 tablespoons butter, melted and divided

½ teaspoon ground cinnamon

1 can (8 ounces) pineapple rings in unsweetened juice, drained

Frozen unsweetened dark cherries, thawed

2 eggs

1 cup low-fat buttermilk

½ cup no-sugar-added pineapple fruit spread

1½ cups all-purpose flour

1 teaspoon baking powder

½ teaspoon baking soda

¼ teaspoon salt

Preheat oven to 350°F. Combine 2 tablespoons melted butter and cinnamon; mix well. Spread onto bottom of 8-inch square baking dish. Top with pineapple rings; place cherries in centers of rings. Beat eggs in medium bowl; blend in buttermilk, fruit spread and remaining ¼ cup butter. Combine flour, baking powder, baking soda and salt. Gradually add to buttermilk mixture, beating until well blended. Spread batter evenly over fruit. Bake 30 minutes or until toothpick inserted into center comes out clean. Cool in baking dish on wire rack 30 minutes. Invert onto serving platter; remove dish. Serve warm or at room temperature.

Makes 6 servings

helpful hint

If you don't have buttermilk, combine 1 tablespoon lemon juice or vinegar plus milk to equal 1 cup. Stir; let stand 5 minutes.

cocoa cheesecake

Graham Crust (recipe follows)

2 packages (8 ounces each) cream cheese, softened

¾ cup plus 2 tablespoons sugar, divided

½ cup HERSHEY'S Cocoa

2 teaspoons vanilla extract, divided

2 eggs

1 container (8 ounces) dairy sour cream

Fresh fruit, sliced

1. Prepare Graham Crust. Heat oven to 375°F.

2. Beat cream cheese, ¾ cup sugar, cocoa and 1 teaspoon vanilla in large bowl until well blended. Add eggs; blend well. Pour batter into prepared Graham Crust.

3. Bake 20 minutes. Remove from oven; cool 15 minutes. Increase oven temperature to 425°F.

4. Stir together sour cream, remaining 2 tablespoons sugar and remaining 1 teaspoon vanilla in small bowl until smooth; spread evenly over top of cheesecake.

5. Bake 10 minutes; remove from oven. Loosen cheesecake from side of pan; cool to room temperature. Refrigerate several hours or overnight; remove side of pan. Garnish with fresh fruit. Cover; refrigerate leftover cheesecake. *Makes 10 to 12 servings*

Graham Crust: Combine 1½ cups graham cracker crumbs, ⅓ cup sugar and ⅓ cup melted butter or margarine in small bowl. Press mixture onto bottom and halfway up side of 9-inch springform pan.

Chocolate Lover's Cheesecake: Prepare batter as directed above; stir 1 cup HERSHEY'S Semi-Sweet Chocolate Chips into batter before pouring into crust. Bake and serve as directed.

cocoa cheesecake

kathy's key lime pie

1 package (8 ounces) cream cheese, softened

1 package (4-serving size) lime-flavored gelatin

2 containers (8 ounces each) frozen nondairy whipped topping, thawed

1 (9-inch) graham cracker crust

1. Beat cream cheese, gelatin and two-thirds of whipped topping in large bowl with electric mixer at medium speed until smooth.

2. Spoon into pie crust; top with remaining whipped topping. Serve immediately or refrigerate until ready to serve. Garnish as desired. *Makes 8 servings*

mixed berry cobbler

1 package (16 ounces) frozen mixed berries

¾ cup granulated sugar

2 tablespoons quick-cooking tapioca

2 teaspoons grated fresh lemon peel

1½ cups all-purpose flour

½ cup packed brown sugar

2¼ teaspoons baking powder

¼ teaspoon ground nutmeg

¾ cup milk

⅓ cup butter or margarine, melted

Ice cream (optional)

Slow Cooker Directions

1. Stir together berries, granulated sugar, tapioca and lemon peel in slow cooker.

2. Combine flour, brown sugar, baking powder and nutmeg in medium bowl. Add milk and butter; stir just until blended. Drop spoonfuls on top of berry mixture.

3. Cover; cook on LOW 4 hours. Uncover; let stand about 30 minutes. Serve with ice cream, if desired.

Makes 8 servings

Prep Time: 10 minutes
Cook Time: 4 hours
Stand Time: 30 minutes

kathy's key lime pie

coconut-topped brownies

1 package (19 to 21 ounces) brownie mix, plus ingredients to prepare

½ cup semisweet chocolate chunks or chocolate chips

½ cup packed brown sugar

2 tablespoons butter or margarine, softened

1 tablespoon all-purpose flour

⅔ cup chopped pecans

⅔ cup flaked coconut

1. Preheat oven to 350°F. Grease 13×9-inch baking pan.

2. Prepare brownie mix according to package directions; stir in chocolate chunks. Spread into prepared pan.

3. Combine brown sugar, butter and flour in small bowl. Mix until well blended. Stir in pecans and coconut. Sprinkle mixture over batter. Bake 28 to 30 minutes or until topping is lightly browned. Cool completely in pan. Cut into bars.

Makes 30 brownies

coconut-topped brownies

famous tiramisu dessert recipe

3 large eggs, separating whites and yolks

1 cup espresso or strong coffee

½ cup sugar

2 tablespoons cognac or brandy

8 ounces BELGIOIOSO® Mascarpone

20 ladyfingers (toasted)

⅛ cup cocoa

Combine 3 egg yolks, 1 tablespoon espresso, sugar, and cognac into large mixing bowl. Beat 2 to 3 minutes. Add BelGioioso Mascarpone and beat 3 to 5 minutes until consistency is smooth.

In another bowl, combine 3 egg whites and a pinch of sugar. Beat until mixture forms stiff peaks. Gently fold into Mascarpone mixture.

Pour rest of espresso into flat dish, dip one side of each ladyfinger, and layer on bottom of serving dish. Spread ½ of Mascarpone mixture and sprinkle with cocoa. Layer ladyfingers and finish with a Mascarpone layer and cocoa. Refrigerate at least 1 hour before serving.

Makes 6 servings

chocolate peanut butter pie

1 can (14 ounces) sweetened condensed milk

¼ cup creamy peanut butter

2 tablespoons unsweetened cocoa powder

1 container (8 ounces) nondairy frozen whipped topping, thawed

1 (6-ounce) chocolate cookie crumb crust

1. Beat condensed milk, peanut butter and cocoa in large bowl with electric mixer until smooth and well blended. Fold in whipped topping. Pour mixture into crust.

2. Freeze at least 6 hours or overnight. Garnish as desired.

Makes 7 to 8 servings

raspberry almond trifles

2 cups whipping cream

¼ cup plus 1 tablespoon raspberry liqueur or orange juice, divided

1 (14-ounce) can EAGLE BRAND® Sweetened Condensed Milk (NOT evaporated milk)

2 (3-ounce) packages ladyfingers, separated

1 cup seedless raspberry jam

½ cup sliced almonds, toasted

1. In large mixing bowl, beat whipping cream and 1 tablespoon liqueur until stiff peaks form. Fold in Eagle Brand; set aside.

2. Layer bottom of 12 (4-ounce) custard cups or ramekins with ladyfingers. Brush with some remaining liqueur. Spread half of jam over ladyfingers. Spread evenly with half of cream mixture; sprinkle with half of almonds. Repeat layers with remaining ladyfingers, liqueur, jam, cream mixture and almonds. Cover and chill 2 hours. Store covered in refrigerator.

Makes 12 servings

Prep Time: 20 minutes
Chill Time: 2 hours

chocolate truffle cups

1 (7-ounce) cup ALOUETTE® Crème Fraîche

8 ounces good quality white or bittersweet chocolate broken into small pieces

1 tablespoon liqueur, such as almond, coffee or orange (optional)

1 (2-ounce) package frozen mini phyllo shells

Heat crème fraîche over medium heat until it softens to a thick liquid consistency. Remove from heat and add chocolate. Stir until chocolate is melted and mixture is smooth. Add liqueur if desired. Refrigerate for 1 hour or until set. Pipe into phyllo shells and serve.

Makes 15 dessert cups

raspberry almond trifles

angel food roll with strawberry sauce

1 box (16 ounces) angel food cake mix

¼ cup plus 2 tablespoons powdered sugar

1 quart strawberry low-fat frozen yogurt

1 container (10 ounces) frozen sliced strawberries with sugar, thawed

1 tablespoon lemon juice

1½ teaspoons cornstarch

helpful hint

To quickly soften frozen yogurt, place in microwave for 15 to 20 seconds.

1. Preheat oven to 350°F. Line bottom of 15×10-inch jelly-roll pan with waxed paper. Prepare cake mix according to package directions; pour evenly into prepared pan. Bake about 20 minutes or until cake is golden brown and springs back when lightly touched.

2. Cool on wire rack 15 minutes. Lay clean kitchen towel on flat surface. Sift ¼ cup powdered sugar over towel; invert cake on top of sugar. Carefully peel off waxed paper. Starting at short end, roll cake up with towel, jelly-roll style. Cool 30 minutes, seam side down, on wire rack.

3. While cake is cooling, remove frozen yogurt from freezer to soften. Carefully unroll cake. Using rubber spatula, place spoonfuls of frozen yogurt on top of cake; spread to edges with table knife. Reroll filled cake; cover tightly with plastic wrap. Freeze at least 3 hours or overnight.

4. To prepare strawberry sauce, combine strawberries, lemon juice and cornstarch in small saucepan; bring to a boil over medium heat. Reduce heat to low; cook and stir 2 to 3 minutes until sauce has thickened. Let cool; refrigerate until ready to serve.

5. To complete recipe, remove cake from freezer 15 minutes before serving. Dust with remaining 2 tablespoons powdered sugar. Cut into slices with serrated knife; serve with strawberry sauce.

Makes 8 servings

Make-Ahead Time: at least 3 hours or up to 24 hours before serving
Final Prep Time: 20 minutes

angel food roll with strawberry sauce

cashew-lemon shortbread cookies

½ cup roasted cashews

1 cup (2 sticks) butter, softened

½ cup sugar

2 teaspoons lemon extract

1 teaspoon vanilla

2 cups all-purpose flour

Additional sugar

1. Preheat oven to 325°F. Place cashews in food processor; process until finely ground. Add butter, sugar, lemon extract and vanilla; process until well blended. Add flour; process using on/off pulses until dough is well blended and begins to form a ball.

2. Shape dough into 1½-inch balls; roll in additional sugar. Place about 2 inches apart on ungreased baking sheets; flatten.

3. Bake cookies 17 to 19 minutes or just until set and edges are lightly browned. Remove cookies from baking sheets to wire racks to cool.

Makes 2 to 2½ dozen cookies

Prep and Bake Time: 30 minutes

chocolate chunk cookies

3 eggs

1 cup vegetable oil

¾ cup packed brown sugar

1 teaspoon baking powder

1 teaspoon vanilla

¼ teaspoon baking soda

¼ teaspoon salt

2½ cups all-purpose flour

1 package (12 ounces) semisweet chocolate chunks

Preheat oven to 350°F. Lightly grease cookie sheets or line with parchment paper. Beat eggs in large bowl until foamy. Add oil and brown sugar; beat until light and frothy. Blend in baking powder, vanilla, baking soda and salt. Mix in flour until dough is smooth. Stir in chocolate chunks. Shape dough into walnut-sized balls. Place 2 inches apart on prepared cookie sheets. Bake 10 to 12 minutes or until lightly browned. Remove to wire racks to cool. *Makes about 4½ dozen cookies*

cashew-lemon shortbread cookies

mini chocolate cheesecakes

3 packages (8 ounces
    each) cream cheese,
    softened

½ cup sugar

3 eggs

1 teaspoon vanilla

8 squares (1 ounce each)
    semisweet baking
    chocolate

helpful hint

*To easily soften cream
cheese, place completely
unwrapped packages of
cream cheese on a
microwavable plate.
Microwave on HIGH 15
to 20 seconds or until
cream cheese is slightly
softened.*

1. Preheat oven to 325°F. Lightly grease 12 (2¾-inch) muffin pan cups; set aside.

2. Beat cream cheese and sugar about 2 minutes in large bowl with electric mixer at medium speed until light and fluffy. Add eggs and vanilla; beat about 2 minutes until well blended.

3. Place chocolate in 1-cup microwave-safe bowl. Microwave at HIGH 1 to 1½ minutes or until chocolate is melted, stirring after 1 minute. Beat melted chocolate into cream cheese mixture until well blended.

4. Divide mixture evenly among prepared muffin cups. Place muffin pan in larger baking pan; place on oven rack. Pour warm water into larger pan to depth of ½ to 1 inch. Bake cheesecakes 30 minutes or until edges are dry and centers are almost set. Remove muffin pan from water. Cool cheesecakes completely in muffin pan on wire rack. *Makes 12 servings*

Mini Swirl Cheesecakes: Before adding chocolate to batter in mixer bowl, place about 2 heaping tablespoons of batter into each muffin cup. Add chocolate to remaining batter in mixer bowl and beat to combine. Spoon chocolate batter on top of vanilla batter in muffin cups. Swirl with a knife before baking.

Reese's® peanut butter and milk chocolate chip studded oatmeal cookies

1 cup (2 sticks) butter or margarine, softened

1 cup packed light brown sugar

⅓ cup granulated sugar

2 eggs

1½ teaspoons vanilla extract

1½ cups all-purpose flour

1 teaspoon baking soda

½ teaspoon salt

½ teaspoon ground cinnamon (optional)

2½ cups quick-cooking oats

1¾ cups (11-ounce package) REESE'S® Peanut Butter and Milk Chocolate Chips

1. Heat oven to 350°F.

2. Beat butter, brown sugar and granulated sugar in bowl until creamy. Add eggs and vanilla; beat well. Combine flour, baking soda, salt and cinnamon, if desired; add to butter mixture, beating well. Stir in oats and chips (batter will be stiff). Drop by rounded teaspoons onto ungreased cookie sheet.

3. Bake 10 to 12 minutes or until lightly browned. Cool 1 minute; remove from cookie sheet to wire rack.

Makes about 4 dozen

Bar Variation: Spread batter into lightly greased 13×9×2-inch baking pan or 15½×10½×1-inch jelly-roll pan. Bake at 350°F. for 20 to 25 minutes or until golden brown. Cool; cut into bars. Makes about 3 dozen bars

Reese's® peanut butter and milk chocolate chip studded oatmeal cookies

brownie baked alaskas

2 purchased brownies
   (2½ inches square)

2 scoops fudge swirl ice
   cream or favorite
   flavor

⅓ cup semisweet
   chocolate chips

2 tablespoons light corn
   syrup or milk

2 egg whites

¼ cup sugar

helpful hint

*When a recipe calls for
sugar, add it slowly to the
egg whites, beating well
after each addition. If the
mixture feels grainy to
the touch, continue
beating before adding
more. If the egg whites
are to be folded into
other ingredients, this
should be done
immediately after they
are beaten.*

1. Preheat oven to 500°F. Place brownies on small cookie sheet; top each with scoop of ice cream and place in freezer.

2. Melt chocolate chips in small saucepan over low heat. Stir in corn syrup; set aside and keep warm.

3. Beat egg whites to soft peaks in small bowl. Gradually beat in sugar; continue beating until stiff peaks form. Spread egg white mixture over ice cream and brownies with small spatula. (Ice cream and brownies should be completely covered with egg white mixture.)

4. Bake 2 to 3 minutes or until meringue is golden. Spread chocolate sauce on serving plates; place baked Alaskas over sauce. *Makes 2 servings*

brownie baked alaskas

chocolate caramel brownies

1 package
(18.25 ounces)
chocolate cake mix

1 cup chopped nuts

½ cup (1 stick) butter or
margarine, melted

1 cup NESTLÉ®
CARNATION®
Evaporated Milk,
divided

35 (10-ounce package)
caramels,
unwrapped

2 cups (12-ounce
package) NESTLÉ®
TOLL HOUSE®
Semi-Sweet
Chocolate Morsels

PREHEAT oven to 350°F.

COMBINE cake mix and nuts in large bowl. Stir in butter and ⅔ *cup* evaporated milk (batter will be thick). Spread *half* of batter into greased 13×9-inch baking pan.

BAKE for 15 minutes.

HEAT caramels and *remaining* evaporated milk in small saucepan over low heat, stirring constantly, until caramels are melted. Sprinkle morsels over brownie; drizzle with caramel mixture.

DROP *remaining* batter by heaping teaspoon over caramel mixture.

BAKE for 25 to 30 minutes or until center is set. Cool in pan on wire rack. *Makes 24 brownies*

chocolate frosted peanut butter cupcakes

⅓ cup creamy or chunky reduced-fat peanut butter

⅓ cup butter, softened

½ cup granulated sugar

¼ cup packed brown sugar

2 eggs

1 teaspoon vanilla

1¾ cups all-purpose flour

1½ teaspoons baking powder

¼ teaspoon salt

1¼ cups milk

Peanut Butter Chocolate Frosting (page 298)

1. Preheat oven to 350°F. Line 18 (2½-inch) muffin cups with foil baking cups.

2. Beat peanut butter and butter in large bowl with electric mixer at medium speed until smooth; beat in sugars until well mixed. Beat in eggs and vanilla.

3. Combine flour, baking powder and salt in medium bowl. Add flour mixture to peanut butter mixture alternately with milk, beginning and ending with flour mixture.

4. Pour batter into prepared muffin cups. Bake 23 to 25 minutes or until cupcakes spring back when touched and toothpick inserted into centers comes out clean. Cool in pans on wire racks 10 minutes; remove from pans and cool completely.

5. Prepare Peanut Butter Chocolate Frosting. Frost each cupcake with about 1½ tablespoons frosting. Garnish as desired.   *Makes 1½ dozen cupcakes*

continued on page 298

chocolate frosted peanut butter cupcakes

chocolate frosted peanut butter cupcakes, continued

helpful hint

If you don't have muffin pans, don't worry. Foil baking cups are sturdy enough to be used without muffin pans; simply place the baking cups on a baking sheet and fill.

peanut butter chocolate frosting

4 cups powdered sugar

1/3 cup unsweetened cocoa powder

4 to 5 tablespoons milk, divided

3 tablespoons creamy peanut butter

Combine powdered sugar, cocoa, 4 tablespoons milk and peanut butter in large bowl. Beat with electric mixer at low speed until smooth, scraping bowl frequently. Beat in additional 1 tablespoon milk until of desired spreading consistency.

Makes about 2 1/2 cups frosting

white chocolate chunk brownies

4 squares (1 ounce each) unsweetened chocolate, coarsely chopped

1/2 cup (1 stick) butter

2 large eggs

1 1/4 cups sugar

1 teaspoon vanilla

1/2 cup all-purpose flour

1/2 teaspoon salt

6 ounces white baking bar, cut into 1/4-inch pieces

1/2 cup coarsely chopped walnuts (optional)

Preheat oven to 350°F. Grease 8-inch square baking pan; set aside.

Melt unsweetened chocolate and butter in small saucepan over low heat, stirring constantly; set aside.

Beat eggs in large bowl with electric mixer at medium speed 30 seconds. Gradually add sugar, beating at medium speed about 4 minutes until very thick and lemon-colored.

Beat in chocolate mixture and vanilla. Beat in flour and salt at low speed just until blended. Stir in baking bar pieces and walnuts, if desired. Spread batter evenly into prepared baking pan.

Bake 30 minutes or until edges just begin to pull away from sides of pan and center is set.

Remove pan to wire rack; cool completely. Cut into 2-inch squares. *Makes 16 brownies*

chewy chocolate macaroons

5⅓ cups MOUNDS®
    Sweetened Coconut
    Flakes

½ cup HERSHEY'S
    Cocoa

1 can (14 ounces)
    sweetened
    condensed milk (not
    evaporated milk)

2 teaspoons vanilla
    extract

About 24 red candied
    cherries, halved
    (optional)

1. Heat oven to 350°F. Generously grease cookie sheet.

2. Stir together coconut and cocoa in large bowl; stir in sweetened condensed milk and vanilla until well blended. Drop by rounded teaspoons onto prepared cookie sheet. Press cherry half into center of each cookie, if desired.

3. Bake 8 to 10 minutes or until almost set. Immediately remove from cookie sheet to wire rack. Cool completely. Store loosely covered at room temperature.   *Makes about 4 dozen cookies*

Prep Time: 15 minutes
Bake Time: 8 minutes
Cool Time: 1 hour

chewy chocolate macaroons

chocolate-berry cheesecake

1 cup chocolate wafer crumbs

1 container (12 ounces) fat-free cream cheese

1 package (8 ounces) reduced-fat cream cheese

⅔ cup sugar

½ cup cholesterol-free egg substitute

3 tablespoons fat-free (skim) milk

1¼ teaspoons vanilla

1 cup mini semisweet chocolate chips

2 tablespoons raspberry all-fruit spread

2 tablespoons water

2½ cups fresh strawberries, hulled and halved

1. Preheat oven to 350°F. Spray bottom of 9-inch springform pan with nonstick cooking spray.

2. Press chocolate wafer crumbs firmly onto bottom of prepared pan. Bake 10 minutes. Remove from oven; cool. *Reduce oven temperature to 325°F.*

3. Combine cheeses in large bowl with electric mixer. Beat at medium speed until well blended. Beat in sugar until well blended. Beat in egg substitute, milk and vanilla until well blended. Stir in mini chips with spoon. Pour batter into pan.

4. Bake 40 minutes or until center is set. Remove from oven; cool 10 minutes in pan on wire rack. Carefully loosen cheesecake from edge of pan. Cool completely.

5. Remove side of pan from cake. Blend fruit spread and water in medium bowl until smooth. Add strawberries; toss to coat. Arrange strawberries on top of cake. Refrigerate 1 hour before serving. Garnish with fresh mint, if desired. *Makes 16 servings*

chocolate-berry cheesecake

lemon melts

½ cup canola oil

½ cup (1 stick) butter, melted

½ cup packed brown sugar

½ cup powdered sugar

1 tablespoon lemon juice

1 tablespoon vanilla

1½ teaspoons almond extract

2 cups all-purpose flour

½ teaspoon cream of tartar

½ teaspoon baking soda

1. Preheat oven to 350°F. Grease cookie sheets.

2. Beat oil, butter, sugars, lemon juice, vanilla and almond extract in large bowl with electric mixer at medium speed until creamy.

3. Combine flour, cream of tartar and baking soda in separate bowl. Gradually beat into butter mixture until stiff dough forms.

4. Drop dough by rounded tablespoonfuls 2 inches apart onto prepared cookie sheets; flatten gently with fork. Bake 20 minutes or until cookies brown around edges only. Cool cookies on cookie sheets 1 minute. Remove to wire racks; cool completely.

Makes about 40 cookies

easy no-bake cocoa oatmeal cookies

2 cups sugar

½ cup unsweetened cocoa powder

½ cup flaked coconut (optional)

½ cup milk

½ cup creamy peanut butter

½ teaspoon vanilla

2 cups uncooked old-fashioned oats

1. Combine sugar, cocoa, coconut, if desired, milk, peanut butter and vanilla in medium saucepan over medium-high heat. Bring to a boil. Stir in oats; mix well.

2. Drop dough by tablespoonfuls onto plates or trays that fit in freezer. Freeze 1 to 2 hours; store in refrigerator until ready to serve.

Makes 2 dozen cookies

lemon melts

cinnamon pear crisp

8 medium pears, cored, peeled and sliced

¾ cup frozen unsweetened apple juice concentrate, thawed

½ cup golden raisins

¼ cup plus 3 tablespoons all-purpose flour, divided

1 teaspoon ground cinnamon

⅓ cup uncooked quick oats

3 tablespoons packed dark brown sugar

3 tablespoons margarine, melted

1. Preheat oven to 375°F. Spray 11×7-inch baking dish with nonstick cooking spray. Set aside.

2. Combine sliced pears, apple juice concentrate, raisins, 3 tablespoons flour and cinnamon in large bowl; mix well. Spoon mixture into prepared baking dish.

3. Combine remaining ¼ cup flour, oats, brown sugar and margarine in medium bowl; mix until coarse crumbs form. Sprinkle evenly over pear mixture. Bake 1 hour or until golden brown. Cool in pan on wire rack.

Makes 12 (½-cup) servings

helpful hint

Store leftover crisps in the refrigerator for up to two days. Reheat them, covered, in a 350°F oven until warm.

cheesecake-filled strawberries

1 package (8 ounces)
    cream cheese,
    softened

1½ tablespoons powdered
    sugar

1½ teaspoons vanilla

1 pint strawberries

1 package (8 ounces)
    sliced almonds,
    toasted

helpful hint

*Strawberries can also be
filled by cutting a wedge
out of the side of each
berry and scooping out
pulp, leaving about
¼-inch shell. Fill and
arrange as shown in
photo.*

1. Beat cream cheese 2 to 3 minutes in medium bowl with electric mixer at medium speed. Add powdered sugar and vanilla; beat until well blended.

2. Trim bottom of strawberries. Scoop out pulp, leaving ¼-inch shell; fill with cream cheese mixture. Top each strawberry with 2 toasted almonds.

3. Place strawberries on serving plate. Refrigerate until ready to serve.   *Makes 4 to 6 servings*

cheesecake-filled strawberries

black forest cake

1 package (18¼ ounces)
    chocolate cake mix
    plus ingredients to
    prepare mix

2 cans (20 ounces each)
    cherry pie filling

Frosting (recipe
    follows)

1. Preheat oven to 350°F. Grease and flour a 17×11-inch jelly roll pan; set aside. Prepare cake mix according to package directions. Pour into prepared pan.

2. Bake 10 to 12 minutes or until wooden toothpick inserted into center comes out clean. Cool in pan on wire rack 20 minutes.

3. Meanwhile, drain cherries. Prepare frosting.

4. Using a 2½-inch cookie cutter, cut 15 circles from cake. Place unused cake in a food processor and pulse several times until cake is breadcrumb texture. Set aside.

5. Reserve 1½ cups frosting for decorating cakes; set aside. Place 1 cake layer on plate. Top with cherries. Repeat two more times to form a three-layer cake. Repeat with remaining circles to form 5 cakes.

6. Frost sides and top of cake. Pat reserved cake crumbs onto frosting on sides of cake. Spoon reserved frosting into pastry bag fitted with star decorating tip. Pipe around edge of cake. Spoon remaining cherries on top.   *Makes 5 cakes*

Frosting: Beat together 3 cups cold whipping cream and ⅓ cup powdered sugar in chilled deep medium bowl with electric mixer at high speed until stiff peaks form.

black forest cake

golden raisin cookies

1½ cups sugar

1 cup (2 sticks) butter, softened

1 tablespoon lemon juice

2 eggs

3½ cups all-purpose flour

1½ teaspoons cream of tartar

1½ teaspoons baking soda

1 package (15 ounces) golden raisins (about 2½ cups)

1. Preheat oven to 400°F.

2. Beat sugar and butter with electric mixer at medium speed until creamy. Add lemon juice. Beat in eggs, one at a time, beating until fluffy.

3. Combine flour, cream of tartar and baking soda in separate bowl; gradually stir flour mixture into sugar mixture. Stir in raisins.

4. Shape into 1-inch balls; place 2 inches apart on *ungreased* cookie sheets. Flatten with floured fork. Bake 8 to 10 minutes or until lightly browned. Cool on cookie sheets 1 minute. Remove to wire racks; cool completely. *Makes about 6 dozen cookies*

chocolate-dipped almond crescents

1 cup butter, softened

1 cup powdered sugar

2 egg yolks

2½ cups all-purpose flour

1½ teaspoons almond extract

1 cup (6 ounces) semisweet chocolate chips

Preheat oven to 375°F. Line cookie sheets with parchment paper or leave ungreased. Cream butter, sugar and egg yolks in large bowl. Beat in flour and almond extract until well mixed. Shape dough into 1-inch balls. (If dough is too soft to handle, cover and refrigerate until firm.) Roll balls into 2-inch-long ropes, tapering both ends. Curve ropes into crescent shapes. Place 2 inches apart on cookie sheets. Bake 8 to 10 minutes or until set, but not browned. Remove to wire racks to cool. Melt chocolate chips in top of double boiler over hot, not boiling, water. Dip one end of each crescent in melted chocolate. Place on waxed paper; cool until chocolate is set.

Makes about 5 dozen cookies

fabulous blonde brownies

1¾ cups all-purpose flour

1 teaspoon baking powder

¼ teaspoon salt

1 cup (6 ounces) white chocolate chips

1 cup (4 ounces) blanched whole almonds, coarsely chopped

1 cup toffee baking pieces

1½ cups packed light brown sugar

⅔ cup butter, softened

2 eggs

2 teaspoons vanilla

helpful hint

For easy removal of brownies and bar cookies (and no clean-up!), line the baking pan with foil and leave at least 3 inches hanging over each end. Use the foil to lift out the treats, place them on a cutting board and simply cut them into pieces.

Preheat oven to 350°F. Lightly grease 13×9-inch baking pan.

Combine flour, baking powder and salt in small bowl; mix well. Combine white chocolate chips, almonds and toffee pieces in medium bowl; mix well.

Beat brown sugar and butter in large bowl with electric mixer at medium speed until light and fluffy. Beat in eggs and vanilla. Add flour mixture; beat at low speed until well blended. Stir in ¾ cup of white chocolate chip mixture. Spread evenly in prepared pan.

Bake 20 minutes. Immediately sprinkle remaining white chocolate chip mixture evenly over brownies. Press lightly. Bake 15 to 20 minutes or until toothpick inserted into center comes out clean. Cool brownies completely in pan on wire rack. Cut into 2×1½ inch bars.   *Makes 3 dozen brownies*

fabulous blonde brownies

ACKNOWLEDGMENTS

The publisher would like to thank the companies and organizations listed below for the use of their recipes and photographs in this publication.

Alouette® Cheese, Chavrie® Cheese, Saladena®

BelGioioso® Cheese, Inc.

Butterball® Turkey

Chef Paul Prudhomme's Magic Seasoning Blends®

Cherry Marketing Institute

Delmarva Poultry Industry, Inc.

Del Monte Corporation

Eagle Brand® Sweetened Condensed Milk

Florida Department of Agriculture and Consumer Services, Bureau of Seafood and Aquaculture

The Golden Grain Company®

Hershey Foods Corporation

The Hidden Valley® Food Products Company

Hormel Foods, LLC

Jennie-O Turkey Store®

Lawry's® Foods

Lee Kum Kee (USA) Inc.

MASTERFOODS USA

McCormick®

Mrs. Dash®

National Honey Board

National Pork Board

National Turkey Federation

Nestlé USA

Norseland, Inc.

Lucini Italia Co.

Perdue Farms Incorporated

Reckitt Benckiser Inc.

The J.M. Smucker Company

TreasureCave® is a registered trademark of ConAgra Brands, Inc.

Unilever Bestfoods North America

Washington Apple Commission

METRIC CONVERSION CHART

VOLUME MEASUREMENTS (dry)

$^1/_8$ teaspoon = 0.5 mL
$^1/_4$ teaspoon = 1 mL
$^1/_2$ teaspoon = 2 mL
$^3/_4$ teaspoon = 4 mL
1 teaspoon = 5 mL
1 tablespoon = 15 mL
2 tablespoons = 30 mL
$^1/_4$ cup = 60 mL
$^1/_3$ cup = 75 mL
$^1/_2$ cup = 125 mL
$^2/_3$ cup = 150 mL
$^3/_4$ cup = 175 mL
1 cup = 250 mL
2 cups = 1 pint = 500 mL
3 cups = 750 mL
4 cups = 1 quart = 1 L

VOLUME MEASUREMENTS (fluid)

1 fluid ounce (2 tablespoons) = 30 mL
4 fluid ounces ($^1/_2$ cup) = 125 mL
8 fluid ounces (1 cup) = 250 mL
12 fluid ounces (1$^1/_2$ cups) = 375 mL
16 fluid ounces (2 cups) = 500 mL

WEIGHTS (mass)

$^1/_2$ ounce = 15 g
1 ounce = 30 g
3 ounces = 90 g
4 ounces = 120 g
8 ounces = 225 g
10 ounces = 285 g
12 ounces = 360 g
16 ounces = 1 pound = 450 g

DIMENSIONS

$^1/_{16}$ inch = 2 mm
$^1/_8$ inch = 3 mm
$^1/_4$ inch = 6 mm
$^1/_2$ inch = 1.5 cm
$^3/_4$ inch = 2 cm
1 inch = 2.5 cm

OVEN TEMPERATURES

250°F = 120°C
275°F = 140°C
300°F = 150°C
325°F = 160°C
350°F = 180°C
375°F = 190°C
400°F = 200°C
425°F = 220°C
450°F = 230°C

BAKING PAN SIZES

Utensil	Size in Inches/Quarts	Metric Volume	Size in Centimeters
Baking or Cake Pan (square or rectangular)	8×8×2	2 L	20×20×5
	9×9×2	2.5 L	23×23×5
	12×8×2	3 L	30×20×5
	13×9×2	3.5 L	33×23×5
Loaf Pan	8×4×3	1.5 L	20×10×7
	9×5×3	2 L	23×13×7
Round Layer Cake Pan	8×1½	1.2 L	20×4
	9×1½	1.5 L	23×4
Pie Plate	8×1¼	750 mL	20×3
	9×1¼	1 L	23×3
Baking Dish or Casserole	1 quart	1 L	—
	1½ quart	1.5 L	—
	2 quart	2 L	—